CHAPTEI

1. TWENTY QUID AND A RUCKSACK
2. WELCOME TO THE PORT
3. THE WHITE PARTY
4. BAR GECKO
5. MY MARRIAGE IS OVER
6. DUQUESA TO LA LINEA
7. EXCITING TIMES AHEAD?
8. THE CAT IS OUT OF THE BAG
9. THE JAZZ SINGER
10. SWEET CAROLINE
11. DEVASTATING NEWS FROM HOME
12. IVAN DRAGO

13 HAS JJ MET HIS TERESA?
14 ROUND TWO DRAGO?
15 SPAIN ISN'T FOR YOU SON
16 GLENN CLOSE
17 BANGED UP ABROAD
18 YOU'RE HAVING A LAUGH, RIGHT?
19 WHAT DOES THE FUTURE HOLD?

There are three sides to every story. There's your side, there's my side and then there's the truth.

Today, you're going to get two sides. Simon's side and the truth...... x

CHAPTER ONE
TWENTY QUID AND A RUCKSACK

JUNE 2018

I can't believe it. I'm actually going to Spain with twenty quid and a rucksack full of clothes. My marriage is over and I'm leaving my two babies behind. What if I fail? What if it doesn't work out? I'm emotionally and physically drained.

"Hello Sir, may I have your Passport and check-in paperwork"?

"Sure".

I hand over my documents to the lassie and she puts my bag on the scale. I've weighed it three times already but I'm shiteing masell in case it comes back overweight. I can hardly afford a pint at this airport never mind an overweight bag.

"That's fine Simon, enjoy your flight Sir"

I head through Security and up to the departure lounge. Look at all those lucky people sitting there drinking their pre-holiday pints. I go to the cash point and take out the only twenty pounds I have to my name and exchange it for Euros. I get twenty-five Euros in return. Bonus.

I'm sat in the departure lounge nervous but excited. I'm contemplating where my sixteen-year relationship and fourteen-year Marriage had gone wrong. Did we just fall out of love? Was it my wife's mental breakdown the Summer before? I'm questioning everything and anything right now.

I get comfortable and facetime the children. They are only nine and thirteen. Aiden and Paige. They are excited to see me go on my new adventure but sad at the same time. I explained to them that I'm doing this so they can come and visit their dad during the school holidays, if I stay.

As I'm on the phone I get a message from my best man from my wedding Ronny. Ronny and I worked together, and he was picked as my best man because he knew the littlest information on my antics pre marriage, and I didn't want to start my wedding on the wrong foot with any crazy stories.

I was also his best man to his second marriage of three. I'll never forget the day of my wedding when my beautiful wife Marie was stood there seven months pregnant with Paige and my best man Ronny was stood at the other side of me. I felt on top of the World.

It felt kinda weird him messaging me quite a bit recently. I kinda distanced myself from him over the past few years as I didn't like the way he had been treating countless women. He was married three times and had multiple affairs after I had picked him as my best man.

When I was young and stupid I sort of thought his behaviour was funny but as I started to get older, I saw that he was actually breaking up multiple families and seemed to get some sort of a kick out of that. Basically, he would've shagged a barber's floor given the chance.

One instance sticks out that when he had been shagging someone's wife, the husband found out about it. The husband hacked into his wife's email account and found a naked photo of him. It wasn't very flattering and luckily there wasn't any pigeons about looking for a tiny wee worm.

The husband cleverly went onto Ronny's social media account. He tagged and told all his friends about his antics with said picture published. Marie and I had a laugh at his wee maggot, and I told her from then that I was going to distance myself from him as this sort of shit was happening too often now. So, I did.

So recently he's sort of came back onto the scene again and has been messaging me. He told that me that he had testicular Cancer and that it had spread and there was not much more they could do, and he was wishing me all the best on my move to Spain.

I felt bad for him. He told me he was caring for his dying Dad and that the Cancer had now taken its toll. He wasn't much older than me, so I felt pretty bad shunning him out for a few years with his antics so decided to be as nice as possible to him due to his struggles.

He was once a really good-looking guy who had the patter to match. Probably why he could pull all the lassies. He never had standards though. If it had a pulse, then he was in there. He didn't care if they were Married, engaged, in a relationship or single. Everything and anything were fair game.

My gate comes up on the screen and head through passport control and get to my gate. Everyone is queuing up already to get on the flight. I don't get that. We're all going to get on you know. I just find a seat and wait until everyone else has boarded and wait until the very end to board.

My work has been fantastic with me. They've given me time off to go and find myself again and told me not to make any rash decisions. My job is here for me when I get back. My plan is to go to Spain for a month. I've already arranged to come back next month and see the kids.

I think I'm just gonna go out there and get a bit of sun and chill out. I'll be back next month. My wife is gonna realise when I'm away that this has all been one big mistake and we'll just get back together as normal and crack on with life as we always did as a family.

I've been invited out to Spain by my Spanish mate Hulio. He knew what had been happening and invited me out to stay for a month with him and his wife. I had stayed in Gibraltar for three years about ten years previously, so I knew the Costa Del Sol well anyway.

He was an odd character. He was a Policeman and a complete pisshead. He smoked massive Cuban Cigars and treated his wife like shit. He was fine with me. I had played football with him a couple of times when I lived in Gibraltar and that's how I knew him, so we kept in touch.

I didn't really know him that well to be honest, but he offered me a haven in Spain to find myself again and I'll forever be appreciative of that. It felt like I was going out to marriage rehab, and I couldn't wait to grasp that with both hands. I had no more tears left to cry.

Hulio knew exactly what I was coming over with, so he had arranged a waiter's job in a local bar in Duquesa port near his home. It would give me some Euros to pay him rent and to save for my trip back to Scotland next month too.

After three hours we arrive in Malaga Airport, and I switch my phone on. I have three messages awaiting me. One from Hulio, one from my kids and another one from my best man.

Hulio – "Hola Amigo, let me know when you land". "I'm at a local Café". I'll drive round to the front of arrivals when you get here". "Saves on parking ha ha".

Kids – "Good luck on your new adventure Dad". "Facetime us tonight when you arrive at your friend's house". "We both miss you so much already" "Paige and Aiden".

Ronny – "Let me know when you arrive in Spain pal". "You're making the right decision here trust me". "I'm proud of you".

Three nice messages to get off the flight to so I reply to all three. Hulio finishes his Coffee and heads round to arrivals to pick me up. I walk outside of the arrivals hall and get hit with a massive gust of heat. I've missed this. Gibraltar and the Costa was amazing back in the day.

I feel like I'm home here it's weird. Is this what's meant to be for me? Suddenly my mood has changed. All of my anxiety I had has gone. That empty feeling in my stomach is gone too. I feel like a new man. I put my Sunglasses on and see this big white car come tearing round the corner with Spanish music blaring out the open windows. It's Hulio.

"Simon my man"! "Throw your rucksack on the back seat and jump in". "Are you ready for the adventure of a lifetime"? He says

"Oh, absolutely pal, I can't wait".

"Ok man, we're about fifty minutes away from Duquesa so just sit back and relax and enjoy the Spanish music and take in the views". A lot has changed since you were last here my man, but you'll get back up to speed in no time". "Have you eaten"?

"No not yet Hulio".

"Look, you told me about your money situation and don't worry, I've got you". "We're going to go and see Duncan when we get there in Duquesa Port". "He owns the bar that you're going to be working in so we'll get a bit of lunch, and I'll introduce you ok"?

"Sounds sweet brother".

We drive South down the beautiful Costa Del Sol. I'd driven this road a million times before with Marie and Paige when she was a baby over here. It all felt a bit surreal being back. I knew that it was going to be for a month. Marie will definitely change her mind when I get back all tanned and toned.

We pull into Duquesa Port after about fifty minutes. I'd never been here before surprisingly enough. It's on a thirty-minute drive from Gibraltar and I would always drive past it and just head to Estepona. It's a lovely wee Port and Marina. It looks all very English for being in Spain.

"Do you speak Spanish Simon"? asks Hulio

"A wee bit".

"Don't worry about it". "Literally everybody in this Port speaks English but try to learn Spanish as you go along".

"Yes, I will".

I look out to the Port. Blue skies and roasting hot. This is definitely me, this is where I belong for now. I miss my kids so much already and also my wife. I need to give her the time to think about her decisions. I know that she's going to do the right thing when I get back. I just know it.

CHAPTER TWO
WELCOME TO THE PORT

Hulio gives me a wee tour of the Port. He takes me into a few bars and restaurants and introduces to me to a few people. I get a very strange feeling that the locals aren't too happy to see him but sort of brush it off.

We then head down to Bar Gecko at the very end of the bar. It looks very clean and trendy. There's this chalk white guy with greasy black hair, skinny and genuinely looking like a bag of shite stood outside it.

"Duncan" shouts Hulio

"Hulio" says Ducan back

"You must be Simon"? says Duncan

"Yes, how are you doing Sir"?

We exchange pleasantries and Duncan shows me around. He tells me to have a few days to acclimatise and then I can start on the Monday morning.

"We're having a White part in here tomorrow night guys". "Yous should come" says Duncan

"A White party"? asks Hulio. "The fuck is a white party"?

"Everybody dresses in White" says Duncan. "It's starts at 8 so I'll see you here"? "It gives Simon a chance to meet the rest of the staff too Hulio".

"Yes, Amigo sure". "We'll be there" says Hulio

We then head to the next town of Sabinillas and again hit a couple of bars.
My favourite one is a nice wee chilled bar called "O'Callaghan's". The owner "Rob" is a lovely guy, and it seems to be the best place around here.

For being a Policeman, Hulio clearly isn't giving a fuck about the drink driving laws out here in Spain and I'm starting to get a bit worried.

"What's the plan for the rest of the day then Hulio"? I ask

"Plan"? "We don't make plans out here Amigo". "We'll head back to mine soon and get freshened up and out on the town". "Get pissed and then head to the whore house eventually".

"The whore house"? "Aren't you married Hulio"?

"Yeah, fuck her". "I'm there 3 nights a week, they love me man".

I've only just got here, and I can see already that this cunt is going to be a complete nightmare. No wonder the locals were all giving him funny looks in that last Port. I hope I haven't made one big mistake here. Let's see.

"Right Simon let's get you back to my place and meet the wife". "We'll show you your room". "We'll call it 50 Euros a week for your room and just put it on your tab ok along with these drinks you've had already too".

I'd spoken to this guy about basically everything before coming out here and not once did I pick up a vibe that he was a complete prick. I've been in his company a couple of hours and noticed that he thinks he owns this place and myself already. That will not be happening pal I can assure you.

We head back to his and I finally get to meet his lovely wife, Joanne.

"Hi Simon, it's nice to meet you, I'm Joanne".

"Yeah yeah" says Hulio. "Make him a few Sandwiches and some Coffee will you"? "The poor lad hasn't had a thing to eat yet".

Joanne looks at him, looks at me and then heads into the kitchen.

"Hulio it's alright mate". "I can wait".

"It gives her something to do around this place just leave her to it".

I'm really starting to dislike this guy already and he takes me up to my room and shows me around the apartment.

"Ok mate" says Hulio. "I'll give you an hour to get freshened up and then we'll hit the down". "Don't worry about money like I said earlier". "Just square me up when you start getting paid by Duncan alright"?

"Ermmmm aye, nae bother man".

The hour passes and we head out. Hulio elects to drive the five minutes down to the Port of Duquesa and leave his car there to collect tomorrow. I've been reliably informed that we'll just get taxis for the rest of the night before heading to the whore house and finally some Irish bar.

The rest of the day is spent at various bars. Hulio getting huckled by the owners of most of the bars we go into for unpaid bar bills. This seems to the theme of the day. I'm really getting a sense that this guy isn't liked at all around the local area. Maybe I should get away from him as soon as possible?

The day turns into night and it's now the time I'm dreading. Hulio is very drunk now and declares….

"Time for the whore house Simon let's go".

We get in the Taxi and even he knows him.

"Maluma baby" says the Taxi driver

I ask Hulio what this "Maluma" shit is that everyone has been screaming at him all day everywhere we've went. Unbeknown to me he's the biggest Latino singer on the planet and Hulio seems to think that he's him every time he's pissed and basically the locals are taking the cunt out of him.

We arrive at the whore house and walk in. I notice right away that as soon as we walk in, all the girls pretend that they are looking at their phones.

"Maluma" screams the barman

"Jesus" screams back Hulio. "This is my Amigo Simon from Scotland". "Tell him the pricelist Jesus and don't worry, put everything on my tab".

"Hi Simon, I'm Jesus". "It's 5 Euros a drink for you and Hulio and if you want to get a girl a drink it's 20 Euros for hers". "It's 50 Euros for every 30 minutes with any of the girls in here so take your pick".

"Ermmm, I'm just here for the drinks Jesus". "I think it's just Hulio who's here for both my man".

"Hulio gets his drink and heads to the dancefloor and keeps going up to multiple girls saying, "Maluma is here girls" and they're all cringing. Hulio does what he has to do and the unfortunate girl he picks, heads through to the back with him. A girl approaches me.

"Hey, I'm Fernanda". "How did you end up being friends with Maluma ha ha".

"Ermmm, I'm starting to ask myself that already".

"Can I let you into a secret Maluma's friend"?

"Sure, and sorry, I'm Simon".

"Pleased to meet you Simon". "We all hate him". "He always comes in drunk and talking shit". "He speaks to all the girls like dirt and then one of us has to do the deed". "He's a fat disgusting pig".

"Yes, so I've seen so far, and I can only apologise for his behaviour".

"Oh, it's not your fault". "I can see already that you are a decent man". "Do you want to come and sit with me and friends"?

"Look Fernanda, no offence, but I just want to sit at the bar with Jesus here and chill". "Once Hulio is done, we'll be gone".

Just at that, Hulio comes back through to the dancefloor area looking all proud of himself.

"Have you picked one yet Simon"? "Although you'll probably be getting my sloppy seconds mind ha ha"?

"Ermm I'm alright Hulio honestly man".
"Look, don't be worried about this tab Simon". "I told you man; we'll square it up".

"I'm not worried about that Hulio, it's just really not my thing".

"Shagging beautiful women isn't your thing Simon"?

"Well yes, but without having to pay for it if you get me"?

"We all pay for it in one way or another Amigo".

Hulio gets back up on the dancefloor pulling at different girls and you can tell they all just hate him. I'm sat at the bar pishing myself laughing at him but after another hour or so, he takes another poor girl through the back.

Fernanda keeps coming to check on me at the bar to see if I'm ok, but I just want to get the fuck out of there. We finally depart the whore house and head out into the dark street.

"How are we going to get a taxi from here Hulio"? I ask

"A taxi"? "There's a slip road down the bottom of the road there". "I'll just phone Joanne to come and get us and say the Taxi driver kicked us out and let that daft bint come and get us".

This guy is fucking unbelievable. He's just been to a whore house and he's getting his wife to come and collect us. She eventually arrives and we head home. The dirty bastard doesn't even get a shower and climbs into bed with his wife. Five minutes later, I can hear them shagging.

This isn't the dream beginning I had for my start in Spain. We have to do the whole thing again tonight now at the White party. Will I get sacked before I even start at this bar? This guy is unbelievable, and I really don't want to be associated with him already…..

CHAPTER THREE
THE WHITE PARTY

We get up in the afternoon to poor Joanne making us lunch. Hulio approaches me.

"If she asks, we were at an Irish bar in Estepona then got kicked out of a Taxi which is where she picked us up ok"?

"Ermmmm aye ok mate".

"How many whores did you shag last night Simon"? "I spent a fortune last night". "Just so I can put in on your tab".

"Ermmmm I didn't shag any mate". "I sat with Jesus at the bar all night waiting for you man". "Ask him the next time you're in".

"You're in"? "We're in ye mean"? "Where do you think we're going after the White Party tonight"?

Hulio walks over to Joanne, kisses her and we sit down for lunch.

"Good night last Simon" asks Joanne

"Ermmmm yes". "We went down the Port and then ended up in some Irish bar in Estepona I think it was". "Hulio and the Taxi driver got into some sort of argument on the way home and he kicked us out". "No clue what it was about as they were shouting in Spanish".

Hulio looks at me and winks. I feel fucking terrible man. Most of the afternoon is hanging around the communal pool area and having a few relaxed drinks with Joanne. She's such a nice person.

"Get your White Shirt and White shorts down Simon" says Hulio. "Joanne will iron them for you".

"Ah Joanne, it's sound pal, I can manage".
"Just leave her to do them, she'll be doing mine anyway".

This guy is different level man. I'm used to doing my own stuff and helping my wife around the house. This fat idiot doesn't lift a finger and treats his lovely wife like a piece of shit. I don't know if he's doing it to just try and impress me but it's doing anything but.

Joanne drives us down to the Port and we head in Bar Gecko. The greaseball Duncan greets us at door and as it says on the tin, everyone is dressed in White. The atmosphere is good, and the clientele looks classy. How Hulio gets in here I'll never know.

Everyone is lovely and out the corner of my eye I see this beautiful woman in her 60's constantly staring at me, so I head over towards her.

"Hi, I'm Simon and I'm new here". "I start in here on Monday and I'm staying with Hulio over there and his wife Joanne for now".

The blonde Lady just rolls her eyes.

"I'm Fay, how do you know Hulio"?

I then explain to her that I don't actually know him and had only played football with him a couple of times but had a crash course in the past 24 hours.

"Ok Simon, I'm going to be honest with you ok"? "Be careful around here". "Everybody wants to be your friend one minute and fuck you the next". "Everybody knows everyone so be careful who you tell your business to as well".

"Great advice, I'll keep that in mind".

"We've all heard about you and your wife splitting already and there's lots of beautiful ladies around here for you to pick from so don't worry about that either".

"Oh, that's the last thing on my mind right now Fay ha ha".

I start working the room and start introducing myself to people and mainly just trying to keep out of the way of Hulio to be honest. Who already, is really starting to get on ones Brad Pitts.

Duncan comes and grabs me and starts introducing me to the staff that work there. Some tall English lass called Nathalie who I'm replacing but doesn't know it yet and some Romanian barman named Cristian who seems ok too. I keep getting handed glasses of Champagne and in general, everybody seems lovely. Well, except one person again. Hulio.

"Simon the shagger" he comes over and says in front of everyone

You can literally see people walking away the second he approaches me.

"Let's blow this joint man it's shit" he says

"I'm actually having a good time Hulio". "Nice people".

"Well, you stay here then, and I'll go up the coast shagging". "Only kidding Simon let's go". "The night is young".

I say my goodbyes to everyone and especially to the lovely Fay who whispers in my ear.

"Be careful with him, he's not liked around here".

She then kisses me on the cheek and gives me a lovely smile. We depart and start hitting some bars in and around the Port and to be fair to Hulio, he's introducing me to everyone. Absolutely everyone which is good. Again, he has bar bills to square up in certain bars, but he doesn't give a fuck.

Just as the night is going well it starts to take that sinister turn yet again.

"Right shagger". "Let's get to the whore house and don't be a fanny tonight and get yourself a girl ok"? "I won't put this one on your tab". "It's on me Simon ok"?

"I think I'll just go up the road mate to be honest". "It's been a good night".
Hulio grabs me by the wrist firmly.

"You're my fucking excuse so you're going fucking nowhere ok"?

"Ermmm, you best let go of my fucking wrist pal".

Hulio lets go.

"If you go home then I'll need to come home with you, or she'll start asking questions". "Just be a friend and come with me". "Sit at the bar and drink all night for free if you want". "Just come eh"?

"Will you stop going on about money, whores and all the other shite you keep going on about man it's ridiculous"? "You've got a lovely wife at home for fucks sake"."You aint impressing me man if that's what you're trying to do"?

"Look, last time I'll ask ok"?

"Last time".

We get in the taxi and head to the whore house again for the 2nd night in a row. We walk in the same thing happens yet again. Phones in faces. We go to the bar and order drinks with Jesus and oor Maluma heads to the dancefloor. Fernanda spots me and heads straight over.

"Back again so soon Simon ha ha". "Look, we all know why you're here". "I've told the girls to leave you alone and they will so don't worry".

"Thanks Fernanda I appreciate that". "Can I get you a drink"?

"You do know it's 20 Euros a drink for me Simon"?

"I really don't give a fuck, have as many as you like tonight and your pals". "Party boy over there is paying the tab".

Fernanda orders a drink for her and her friends and then comes back over to me.

"Look Simon, I know you don't want anything but am I ok to sit"?
"Sure, of course you are".

We get talking and she's actually a really nice person. She does this to pay for her studies, and she has a young child too. We're both laughing at Hulio who is making a complete cunt of himself on the dancefloor. After about an hour he comes over all a sweaty mess.

"Who's your friend Simon"? he asks

"This is Fernanda Hulio".

"Fernanda hey"? "Are you new here"? he asks

"Yes, it's my first week" she replies

"I thought I hadn't seen you before". Are you taking this one Simon"?

"No mate, I thought I cleared things up earlier no"?

"Well, if you don't I will".

Hulio takes Fernanda's hand. She finishes the drink that he's paid for but doesn't know it yet and takes the poor girl through the back to pay for her services. Just before she goes through, she looks back at me terrified. The poor girl.

The same shit happens when he's done with the girls but this time, we do get a Taxi back to his, instead of his poor wife coming to collect us this time. I get a shower and hit the sack. I'm contemplating going back to Scotland already.

I'm 40 years old and can't physically keep this sort of lifestyle up. Especially in this heat too. Lack of food and constant alcohol. I'll wait until we get up but tomorrow, I'll be having strong words with Hulio. It's not the start I was hoping for but hopefully things can only get better…..

CHAPTER FOUR
BAR GECKO

I have the man chat with Hulio on the Monday morning as Joanne is at work in Gibraltar and he apologises. He says that he goes back to work today as well as me starting in the bar tonight. He works 4 on and 4 off so doesn't drink when he's working.

He toddles off to Gibraltar after our chat and I head down to the Port to start my first night in the bar.

"Hi Simon" rings out from every fourth or fifth person as I'm strolling through the Port. People are starting to get to know me already which is nice. I head to the bar and Duncan is already there to show me the ropes along with Cristian.

They show me all the procedures with the till and how all the systems work etc and show me the upcoming acts that they have coming to the bar. They have tons of live music from Jazz to Soul acts and apparently, it's the classiest bar in the Port where no dickheads get in, well, barring Hulio.

One the acts coming in over the next few nights is a Jazz singer named Jennifer. On her poster she looks absolutely sensational but what will she see in a broken overweight Scotsman? Yes, my thoughts exactly.

I get off to a great start at Gecko. Bonnie, Nell and Luciano that work in the kitchen are all sound too. It's a really good working environment. Fay has popped in a few times to see me too for a glass of Wine and it's all very chilled. What a difference when Hulio is working. I haven't even seen him.

Duncan asks me when I'd like paid. Weekly or monthly so I chose weekly, so I always had a wee bit of money and the quicker I paid off Hulio the better too. He agrees to pay me weekly. It gets to the night where the jazz singer is playing and I'm nervous.

She arrives and the posters she has up don't actually do her justice. She is even better in person. It takes a lot to blow me away, but this Woman is just essence. She's sweet, classy and beautiful and boy can she sing too. It's far too early for me to even look at another woman so I just introduce myself as she arrives and get on with me duties.

The night goes off perfectly. So chilled on the Port. Jennifer says her goodbyes and we close up for night. Duncan pours me a pint of Peroni, and we chew the fat.

"So, what's the story with Jennifer then Duncan"? I ask

"Oh, she's from New Zealand and lives up in Marbella with her boyfriend".

"Oh right, lucky guy". "She's beautiful".

"Yes, she is and such a nice girl too".

Just my luck I'm thinking. It's early days but I've been completely blown away already by Jennifer. She's obviously out of my league but that's the standard set already.

Can I find anything remotely close to her if things with my wife don't work out? I finish my Beer, say my goodbyes and head outside and Hulio is stood there.

"4th shift finished Simon, let's get a few Beers".

"Ah na man I'm shattered, it's been a long day".

"Shut up, my treat, come on"

Here we go again. Hulio drags me everywhere and we get in a Taxi and he says something to the Taxi driver in Spanish and we're off. Yes, you've guessed it. We end up at the whore house yet again.

This behaviour from him is just on constant repeat. I don't see him for four days and then it's four days of complete carnage and whore houses. It just keeps happening and I'm at the end of my tether really. I'm due to go back to Scotland next week after my month and really can't wait now.

I've been constantly facetiming the kids and haven't spoken to my wife once since I've been away. She doesn't want to come onto the phone to see me. I'm hoping that when I go home next week, we can just patch things up and go back to the way things were. Let's see.

Bonnie, Nell and Luciano can't stand Hulio either. He's constantly in the bar over the next three days talking to everyone like a piece of shit and telling everyone I'm his mate and staying with him at the same time. I can see the tide turning with me and everyone soon too if I don't fix this.

I've been out here nearly a month now and get on so well with everyone, but this guy is ruining everything. Nell pulls me aside in the kitchen.

"Look Simon, if things don't work out when you go back to Scotland next week with your wife and kids, just come back out mate ok"?

"I can't Nell". "I don't think I can spend another second with that prick Hulio".

"Look honey, me and Luciano have been speaking ok"? "We have a spare room at our place down in La Linea". "You can move in with us ok"? "We love you mate"? "We'll bring you here with us for work and take you home with us also". "Sorted".

"Awwww, I really appreciate that Nell I really do but I don't think I'll be back". "I'm going home to sort my marriage out and I miss the kids so much too".

"Well, the offer is there mate ok"?

"I really appreciate it Nell, thank you so much".

Amazing. If I do come back out to Spain, then I get to leave that hellhole of a place with Hulio. His wife is so lovely and doesn't deserve to be treated the way she is or have such a scumbag as a man. I feel terrible lying for him also and it all needs to stop.

I finish the rest of my week, and Duncan tells me that if I want to come back out then my job will be waiting for me but deep down in my heart, I know I'll be staying home with my wife and kids.

I manage to pay Hulio off for the drinks he's bought me and also the imaginary ones he made up too plus pay Joanne the rent for the four weeks that I stayed there. Joanne has also said that my room is there should I need to come back out.

I pack up the same rucksack that I came to Spain with only four weeks previously. I take one last look at my room as I know that I won't be back and Hulio shouts me down as he's taking me to the airport for my flight home.

Hulio has Maluma booming in the car all the way to airport and we finally arrive with my ears ringing to Maluma's greatest hits. Hulio parks up and gets out the car.

"Look mate, I don't know if Joanne said to you or that, but she doesn't really want you at the house for much longer" say Hulio

"Sorry"?

"Like if you come back out". "She thinks you've been there a bit too long now".

"Hulio are you for real man"? "That's not what she just said to me an hour ago"?

"I'm just telling you as a mate". "Hopefully, and don't take this the wrong way but you don't come back out". "You sort things out with your wife and kids". "It's just she's said that maximum two weeks if you do come back out ok"?

"You're fucking unbelievable man" I say

"What"?

"Och, it doesn't matter man".

I head on into the terminal and check in for my flight to Prestwick Airport. My wife is picking me up with the kids and I just can't wait to see the three of them again.

I Facetime the kids who are all excited to see me and head to the bar to get myself a wee Coffee before I get on my flight. My phone goes and it's my best man from my wedding. I haven't heard from him really since I've been in Spain so it's a pretty odd call to receive.

"Hiya pal, how's you"? says Ronny

"Sound mate aye". "Just at Malaga airport". "That's me on my way home to head back to Marie and the kids".

"What"?

"Aye, I was only coming oor for a month". "Mind a telt ye"?

"Aye but are you no staying oor there"? "Ye daft"? "Spain or Scotland"?

"Och, I know but my wife and weins aren't in Spain are they"?

"Do you think you'll be able to patch things up with Marie"?

"Och who knows man". "We've been together 16 years so I'm assuming so".

"Well good luck pal and safe travels home".

"Cheers dude".

What an odd call to get just before I'm about to get on the flight.

I finish my Coffee and head to gate B4. I get on the flight and it's pleasant to hear some Scottish accents again after a month.

I've no clue what I'm heading back to but one thing is for sure, regardless of what happens, my babies are all that matters in all of this.

CHAPTER FIVE
MY MARRIAGE IS OVER

I arrive at Prestwick Airport around 9.20 am and the plan is to get some breakfast in Ayr, do stuff with the kids and then drop them off so that my wife and I can chat in relative peace with no arguments.

It becomes very apparent when I get off the plane from the very second, I set eyes on my wife Marie. My marriage is over.

I just got this cold look from her, and I was expecting the complete opposite. I had re-charged the batteries in Spain. Hit the Gym and was all tanned and toned.

We went for breakfast with the kids in Ayr and headed to Troon for what I thought would be a nice wee family day out. How wrong I could be?

My wife took absolutely no interest in me.

She doesn't want to converse in any way shape or form. I was completely baffled. Was this the same person I had known for sixteen years?

We finished up by playing crazy golf, had a bit of lunch and then ice cream with the kids.

"So, when we going home Marie, I'm a wee bit tired as I was up early and the travel etc darling"?

"Home"? "Me and the kids are going home". "I don't know where you're going".

"Eh"?

"You're not staying with us Simon".

"What are you even going on about Marie"? "We don't need to sleep in the same bed or that if that's what you mean"? "I'll sleep on the couch".

"What part of you're not staying with us do you not get Simon"?

I'm completely baffled. I did not see this coming at all. I thought I was coming home, going to sort everything out and everything would be fine. My fears were confirmed. She dropped me off at Ayr Hospital and my sister hastily arranged a room for me at her place in Kilmarnock to stay.

The next week was completely horrific. I had arranged lots for us to do but after a few days my daughter didn't even want to be in my company. I was completely at a loss and had no clue what was going on.

My boy Aiden and I went on a camping to trip to Edinburgh whilst I weighed up my options.

I didn't even get to chat to Marie at all about anything when I was home and by the end of the week my mind was made up. I had no option really but to back out to Spain and start my life again at forty. I had nothing and lost everything.

I speak to Duncan and Hulio and let them know of my decision when I'm up in Edinburgh. I call Nell and let her know that I'll take her up on the offer of that room in La Linea as well and she's delighted, as is Luciano.

I get round as much of the family as I can when I'm home too and let them know of my decision. The toughest part was going to have to tell the kids. Well, my son. Suddenly, my daughter had completely stopped talking to me.

It was fucking heartbreaking.

I made the best of the time I had home as much as I could. I booked a flight back to Spain for tomorrow and my Wife said that she'd drop me off so that the kids could say goodbye.

She arrived at my sisters to pick me up to take me to the airport. She didn't look at me or say one word to me all the way to the airport. You could cut the tension in the car with a knife. It was horrible. It didn't feel like I was going to start a new life in Spain. It felt like I was being led to the fucking Gas chamber.

We arrive at Prestwick Airport, and I instruct the kids to get out of the car and stand on the pavement so I could give them some hugs before I go and to talk to their Mum for a moment in private. The kids depart the car and stand just outside it on the pavement.

"Marie"

She turns around on her seat and looks me dead in the eye. Her eyes were seriously like Ice. I'd never seen this before.

"You are genuinely making the biggest mistake of your life". "You don't know it just yet but trust me, you are". "I can't thank you enough for this new opportunity". "Best of luck with everything".

She didn't say a word back and I just got out the car. I went into the boot and got my trusted rucksack out yet again. I knew how much it weighed already because I'd weighed it twice already in the past month. I go to each of the kids individually.

"Paige, look after your wee brother for me ok"? "I promise you I'm going to make a life over in Spain not just for me but for you two as well ok"?

She nods, we hug and we're both crying. She goes back into the car.

"Aiden". "You are the man of the house now son ok"? "You turn into a big strong boy like your dad and come and see me for all your school holidays ok mate"?

"Yes Dad".

We hug and I kiss on him the forehead and he gets into the car. My wife couldn't drive away quick enough. I watch my family that I loved and cherished for 16 years drive away with the smell of petrol burning in my nostrils.

I watch the barrier go up and that's it. This is it. No turning back now. I head on into the airport and check in. I head to the Departure Lounge and get close to the gate for Malaga Airport.

I phone Hulio to double check he's picking me up and call Duncan too to let him know that I'll be back in work tomorrow night as normal. I also call Nell to let her know my plan with Hulio and she can't wait to accommodate me.

My phone goes. It's Ronny my best man again.

"You seem to have a habit of calling me when I'm at Airport's man ha ha".

"Och no way, you at the airport aye"?

"Aye mate". "Heading back to Spain man". "Things didn't go to plan with Marie as I thought it would".

"Och no way man"? I thought you were here for another couple of days at least and was gonna meet up".

"Afraid not Amigo, heading back". "The marriage is over".

"Fuck sake man". "So where did you stay then when you were home"?

"Well I thought at my hoose but Marie was having none of it so I had to crash at my sister's"?

"Whit man"? "She didn't even let you at the hoose"?

"Na man nada". "Nowhere near and was as cold as ice the whole time I was back". "Fuck knows what's wrong with her man". "Something definitely up".

"Och there's loads or darlings oot in Spain, I'm sure you'll be fine shagger"?

"Och Ronny I'm genuinely no interested mate". "I thought I'd be coming back to sort things out but it's not to be unfortunately".

"Och just go out there and enjoy life" "All will be good pal".

"Aye cheers mate".

"Nae bother Simon and always here if you need me even though this Cancer is getting worse and my dad is too".

"Och man, I'm gutted I couldn't see you and give your Da my best too".

"Will do, save travels pal".

"Catch ya Ronny".

Poor cunt. I'm absolutely heartbroken for him. His Cancer has spread, and he's got his dying Dad to look after too. I can't imagine how tough it must be for him and here's me feeling all sorry for myself because I've lost my Wife. It pales in significance really.

"Last call for Malaga at gate C2".

"Shit"!

Too busy on the phone to every man and his dug. I head to the gate and get on the plane. It's weird heading back oot to Spain. Everyone getting on is chalk white and I'm the only Scottish person getting on with a tan haha.

I've got a lot to sort out when I get back to Spain. I need to find a way to tell Hulio I'm leaving his gaff. Cristian that works in the bar is also getting on not only my tits but the kitchen staffs too.

He's an arrogant Romanian wank!

This time it's different. I was going out for a month's holiday but now I'm going out to start a completely new life. It's going to be filled with happiness, joy and sadness but I'm excited. Let's get this adventure started…..

CHAPTER SIX
DUQUESA TO LA LINEA

I get back to Spain and Hulio is doing the exact same shit. Working for four days and then getting fucked up and shagging whores. The difference is now. I'm not going with him or being his excuse now and it's making him irate.

"Ermmm Simon". "Joanne keeps asking when you're moving out mate"?

"She is aye"? "Not once has she said a word to me".

"Well yes, she's shy you know".

"I speak with her more than I speak to you". "Me and her get on great".

"You do"?

The plan is all in motion. Hulio is working tonight, and I know he'll be getting ready before Joanne arrives back from work in Gibraltar, so I pick my time very carefully. Luciano drives me up to the gaff to get my stuff.

"Do you need me to come in with you mate in case he kicks off"? asks Luciano

"Ha ha behave man" I say

I head in and he's getting ready in the living room. Putting his Policeman's uniform on that he's not fit for purpose to wear. I head upstairs to my room to grab my stuff that's already packed and head downstairs. He's sat down on his chair putting his shiny Black Boots on and looks up at me.

"I just want to say thank you for putting me up and giving me the opportunity to come out here in the first place". "I will no longer be your excuse to lie to your wife".

"The way you treat that lovely woman is absolutely disgusting by the way". "Even attempt to stand up and I'll put you straight back down".
He sits there looking at me and doesn't move a muscle or say a word.

"Now there's my hand as a man saying thank you".

He shakes my hand, and I leave without him saying a word. It's amazing how different people are when they don't have alcohol in them eh? I load the mighty rucksack into Luciano's car, and we head down to La Linea to my new place with Nell and Luciano and their two dogs.

I get settled into my new room and its fucking bliss. No more walking on eggshells. No more lies and not living under the same roof as the biggest cunt known to man. This is the fresh start I needed and right next to Gibraltar now as well which is in walking distance.

Gibraltar is not only close. It brings fresh opportunities. Maybe I could leave that bar altogether and get a career started in Gibraltar? The world is now my Oyster and I'm finally excited about the future.

I continue to travel up to Duquesa every day with Nell and Luciano for work and keep my job in Gecko. Duncan is worried about Hulio as he doesn't see him as much but is delighted at the same time as he's not in abusing his customer's.

Word quickly gets around the small port that I've left Hulio's place and everyone is delighted. I didn't actually realise how much he was hated around that area until I left and from the outside, I could look in. He started to get barred from some places and then asked me for a chat one day, so I agreed. We went for Coffee in Sabinillas away from the prying eyes of the Port.

"Look Simon I'm sorry man ok"?

"Sorry for what exactly Hulio"?

"I'm a sex addict man and can't help my urges and decisions".

"No fucking shit man"?

"I've maxed out all the credit cards on whores". "I won't be able to keep it from Joanne for much longer mate".

"Well, what the fuck do you want me to do man"? "I'm a waiter on 7 Euros an hour".

"I don't want you to do anything Simon, I'm just telling you". "Explaining my behaviour".

"Well, it's big of you Hulio".

"Can we still be mates"?

"Honestly"? "No". "I don't need or want people like you in my life". "Best of luck".

I stand up and walk away from him. I felt bad but shouldn't have. He needs to address these issues with his wife and not me. The guy is a cunt. Simple. I have no time for them nor invite them into my life anymore. Adios Hulio.

The weeks go by at Gecko and most of the Summer is done now. The only thing I look forward to now is

Jennifer coming to play at the bar. I've never met or seen anything like her to this point, and she is just sensational inside and now but I know I'm still not ready for anybody.

Cristian has really been getting to everyone at the bar all over the Summer now with his attitude and the way he speaks to everyone and pervs on every single woman that comes into the bar also. He's a creep and we confront Duncan about his behaviour.

I, Nell and Luciano summon Duncan for a meeting.

"He goes or us three go" says Luciano

Now Luciano is the head chef and a brilliant one at that. His wife Nell is his assistant, and Bonnie looks after the kitchen. We all genuinely hate him and have been left with no choice but to go to Duncan about him.

"Ok ok" says a pathetic looking Duncan. "I'll let him go".

We all rejoice. It's not easy someone losing their job but it wouldn't surprise me if this guy is some serial sex offender on the run from Romania, he's that bad with the Ladies.

Cristian is told to leave the bar.

The end of the summer is coming so Duquesa is starting to get quiet again. Duncan starts asking us to leave work earlier and earlier as it's quiet. Or so he says. It doesn't bother us. It means that myself, Nell and Luciano can have a couple of drinks in the Port most night's before heading back to La Linea.

One night we get sent home early yet again and head to a local bar. After about an hour so I realise I've left my phone in the kitchen when I was going in to get Nell and Luciano. I walk into Gecko's and who is serving Cocktails behind the bar? Cristian!

I look at Cristian, then look at the drunk and dishevelled Duncan at the end of the bar. I walk into the kitchen to get my phone and head back to the bar to tell Luciano and Nell. The three of us are absolutely fucking fuming. The next day we summon Duncan yet again and ask him what the fuck is going on.

"So, you are sending us home early so you can give that prick shifts aye"? I say to Duncan

"Look it's my business and I can do what I want ok"? he says

"Correct" I say back.

"However, we did say it was him or us" says Luciano

"Yous aren't working with him are yous"? says Duncan

"That's correct also" I said. "I'm out of here you weak little cunt".

Duncan said nothing back.

I walk round the corner to our usual little haunt after work and two minutes later, Nell and Luciano walk in.

"That'll be that then"? says Nell

The three of us quit on the spot and had a shot together to celebrate.

The drive back to La Linea was a joyous one. No more drunken Duncan or sex offender Cristian. It was going to be a fresh start for all three of us in the morning.

The three of us get up in the morning and decide to head to Gibraltar for a day out on the piss. I text a few pals whilst I'm in there as well to see if there's any jobs about and they say that they'll put the feelers out. We get drunk and have a great day and retire back to La Linea.

I spend the next few days heading into Gibraltar for lunch with pals and to chew the fat. A few opportunities come up in no time and a few interviews also. I soon get hooked up with a wee job in Security, looking after a prominent building in Gibraltar.

No more daily commutes up to Duquesa and I've never been happier to leave a place in my life and hopefully never to return. I get out my bed, head to work in Gibraltar, go to the Gym and back to Nell and Luciano's. That's my routine and I love it.

Both kids have stopped talking to me now on Facetime but I'm aware that their mother has had a few months to work on them now so completely understand the situation.

I'm working, training and sleeping. It might sound boring to some, but I was loving life. Seeing the Rock of Gibraltar every single day on the way into work just does something to me that I can't explain. It just fires me up.

I'd been drinking quite a bit over the Summer to get over my marriage collapsing and the children not speaking to me so decided to take part in Sober October to give the Liver a rest too.

There was something missing in my life out here now and I couldn't quite put my finger on it. Was it a woman or was it something else? Little did I know that something magical was about to happen very quickly indeed….

CHAPTER SEVEN
EXCITING TIMES AHEAD

OCTOBER 2018

Sober October started off very boring indeed. What on Earth was I going to do with all this spare pub time I had? I had a bit of a Gambling issue when I lived in Scotland and probably another reason why my wife decided to leave me. It really became a big problem.

I used to go into the bookies and pick up a pen and write my bet out and if it won then I'd keep that pen. If it lost, I'd throw that pen away and get a new one and so on and so on. Madness, eh? It's the pen's fault Simon.

I had this wee story in my head about a guy that came across a lucky Bunnet and every time he had it on his head, magical things happened. His luck completely turned around from the Bookies to the wimmin. He couldn't lose.

I had a few friends that were Author's already so thought, fuck it, and started to write out what was in my head at night in my room when I was bored during sober October. I sent the first chapter off to an Author friend and he loved it and said for me to keep going with it so I did.

One month later I was done. "The Bunnet" was born. I had finished it. This wee magical story was done and I just had to figure out how to get it published and out there for the one or two people to read it. Or so I thought.

I was plodding along with the writing and getting very excited about it as it was unfolding and I was updating my ever-increasing following on social media not only about my escapades in Spain, but my progression in Sober October too.

My following had seen me out literally every day somewhere in Spain living it up and now nothing. I got lots of messages daily in my inbox but one perked my interest. A woman from Glasgow named Sharon. She looked beautiful and fun. We exchanged a few messages over that sober month.

It became apparent that Sharon was a single mother to a teenage boy and had just come out of an abusive relationship with an older man but that her boys Dad was a good man and she was up to date with my situation too and seemed interested.

I still wasn't sure if I was ready to date again or not but this seemed like the perfect opportunity to try. I could go home and see my friends and family and date Sharon too with the possibility of her coming out here as well. The issue being, I didn't have my own place though.

I wouldn't disrespect Nell and Luciano by even asking them to bring a Woman back to their place never mind just doing it. There were no concrete plans for me to go back to Scotland to see Sharon or for her to come to Spain. We just Facetimed most nights and it was genuinely nice.

It was nice to have an amazing woman back in my life and over the next few months she put a smile on my face daily which was nice. I had also worked out how to self-publish a book on Amazon so "The Bunnet" was very close to being released.

I managed to find a proofreader on a Social Media platform who was going to look over it for me and after just under a month or so it was all done. I started writing it at the start of October and it got released onto Amazon on the 29th of October 2018. It was that quick.

The Book went down a storm, especially in my local area. I honestly couldn't believe it. The support from my local area was absolutely incredible and to this day, still is. They really took to it and to see it in the shop window of my local Book shop was madness.

What had happened in my life? What had I become? I hated English at school and the thought of writing anything at school barring my usual 100 lines every day for being naughty was completely out of the question. I couldn't think of anything fucking worse to be honest.

The adulation I was getting back home for the Book was unbelievable and completely unexpected. People that had read it were asking within a week, when the next one was out. It was that crazy. The next one I'm thinking? I didn't think anyone was going to read this one never mind the next one.

I was still in daily contact with Sharon and it was approaching Christmas. Nell and Luciano were going to Canada, back to Luciano's parents' house and I was all alone in Spain with a dog sitter, auld alcoholic Joe. Now don't get me wrong, he was a lovely old guy but drank for England.

It was my first ever Christmas in sixteen years without my wife or my kids and I was utterly devastated. Joe took me to the pub and introduced to me to the who's who of other lonely people from the UK that have made this coast their home. Do you know what? It was a lovely wee day.

Christmas came and went and then completely out of the blue I get a call from Sharon. She used to work for a famous Lawyer in Scotland, and he was having a party at his home in Glasgow to bring the New Year in. I was telling her that she should go. She wanted me to be her plus one and invited me over.

Of course, I said yes and I booked my flights.

I hadn't met her in person, but we had spoken literally every day on video since October, and I couldn't wait to spend some time with her and get to know her. I told my family and friends I'd be back and text my best man Ronny about meeting up too as I'd missed him last time.

I went home and Sharon met me at Glasgow Central, and we drove back to hers. I couldn't take my eyes off her all the way back to hers. I hadn't been with a woman since my wife, so this was all very alien to me again. She looked great and even better in person.

We got back to hers and got to know each other a little and then got ready for the party. She looked sensational in her white dress and I was one lucky man as we set off for the party.

We arrived at the Lawyer's party and to be honest with you. It was so nice to hear those bells and get 2018 out of my life forever. I looked into Sharon's eyes and kissed her and thanked her for putting that smile back onto my face once again.

I was only there for another day and had to fly back home for work, but it was such an amazing few days and Sharon promised to come and see me next time over in Spain which we arranged pretty quickly.

Luciano picked me up at the airport and on the way down to the house in La Linea broke some surprising news to me.

"Ermmm, sorry mate but Nell has got family coming over in March, so we are going to need that room back by then". "We're not kicking you out mate". "It gives you a couple of months".

I was fucking stunned. I was so glad to see the back of 2018 and 2019 starts like this. On the way down the coast, I get a text from my best man too.

"Sorry buddy just seen this, not been doing too good so wouldn't have been able to meet you anyway".

I didn't even reply with the news I just got. It was a pretty silent car journey home. I got back and told Sharon right away who was also fuming. She even suggested just coming home to live with her at one point in Maryhill. My best man was playing on my mind now, so I text him.

"You ok pal"? That's me back in Spain and home".

"Ah good". "I'm going through Girvan next week". "Do you want me to pop in and see the kids for you and make sure they're ok"?

"My kids are fine". "They go to my Mum and Dad's regularly, so I know they're ok". "You haven't even met my kids, so they won't even know who you are so don't bother your arse thanks".

"What's the matter"? "Are you scared me, and Marie will hit it off"?

At that very moment I blocked him on absolutely every device I had so he couldn't contact me. I contacted my Wife to tell her that he had sent me some disturbing messages about going to contact her and go and see the kids etc.

He had gone from being a friend in the past year or so to an interrogator. I only let him back into my life as I felt sorry for the situation he was in. Everything was all very weird, and I couldn't quite put my finger on it at all.

I got a reply from wife about ten minutes later.

"Don't worry about Ronny. He's great with me and he's great with the kids".

BOOM!

The penny finally dropped. The best man from my wedding who stood beside me when my wife was seven months pregnant with our first child was shagging my wife and putting my kids out to school and taking them on day trips.

He was sitting on my couch, holding my remote control and watching the TV and all that I had worked hard and paid for whilst tucking my children in at night and fucking my wife?

I contacted my mother straight away to tell her about the situation, and she was completely stunned. I told her I'd be back home tomorrow and apologised for what was about to happen. What I said will remain between myself and her. She eventually over 24 hours, talked me out of that and I'm glad she did, along with some friends.

I was stunned. Completely stunned. Ronny? The guy we both laughed at with the micro penis photo. The guy who had ruined so many families lives over the years. Was he lying to me all this time about his Cancer and his dad? He was pushing for me to go to Spain and now I know why.

They both even waited until I was back in Spain to drop the bombshell the shitebags. Do yous really wanna take me on? You both should know better than that. Let's go……

CHAPTER EIGHT
THE CAT IS OUT OF THE BAG

It took me a few days to re-group from the shock of what I'd just found out from back home. I spoke to friends over here where similar things had happened to them and as ever, the advice saved me from a murder charge. Once the news spread, I started to get literally hundreds of messages.

Everything was starting to make sense now. My wife would go away for weekends towards the end of our marriage and there would never be any photos of her and her friends on social media from these weekends away which was very odd to me.

Then there were all the messages and calls I would get off Ronny. It wasn't messages or calls that a pal would send you. It felt like an interrogation. Always asking about and the kids. "Heard from Marie"? "Heard from the kids"? Like every single time I spoke with him.

Now we know why…..

So, the messages started flooding in from Women. Exes of his. Not just any exes but ex wives, girlfriends and fiancés. It turned out this dickhead was engaged to three different women at the exact same time. (No joke). The stories of abuse, mental and physical, plus his cheating were filling up my inbox.

It turned out there was a catalogue of reports in against him whilst he was in the military against multiple women, and I was hoping there was a record of them with the civilian Police too. This monster was around my children, and I had to do something and soon.

I genuinely couldn't give a fuck that he was with my ex-wife, my priority was my children. He can do whatever he likes to her. My children though? Not a hope in hell. I contacted Police Scotland to relay my fears of this monster being around my children and they acted quickly.

The children were pulled out of school and interviewed, and I believe their mother was too. Unfortunately, there was no civilian record of this monsters' activities whilst in the military so there was nothing that the civilian Police could do about it.

His crimes were extensive. He even befriended a young vulnerable woman who was actually on suicide watch, and he was the Sergeant assigned to make sure she was ok. Of course, his MO (Modus Operandi) was vulnerable women, so she was perfect for him to prey on and prey on he did.

He started having sex with her. Got engaged to her. Physically and emotionally abused her even breaking a wrist at one point when he threw her down some stairs. This is one of the many girls that contacted me, and she was one of the three girls he was engaged to at the same time.

None of the three of them even knew about each other either.

This was this guy's MO, to lure and groom vulnerable women. He was a professional at it. We counted seventeen women he had been engaged to. Three marriages and three divorces and he had used and abused women all over the UK for his sexual gratification.

When he felt like he was losing a woman he'd play the let's get engaged card. The names in my inbox kept piling up daily and every single one of these women hated this monster and wanted revenge on him for what he had done to each and every single one of them.

The plan was set.

We had around thirty women plus me and one other male friend who had served with him and help put all this together too. Every single person in this group hated this piece of shit for multiple reasons. I must be honest. If I never had children with Marie, then I would've let him destroy her too. That's how I felt at that time. Can you blame me?

My ex-wife's social media was spouting her love for this perfect individual who had her on strings and was telling her everything that she wanted to hear. It was a beautiful love story in the making….

The main girl who he was meant to watching on suicide watch was the main woman in all of this who was now happily married with two children. He always thought that whatever he said or told her to do then she would. He always thought that she'd be that weak and vulnerable little girl.

Oh, how wrong, he was about to find out he was….

The plan was for her to text him and then slowly but surely the other exes would just to see what his response would be. The main woman in all of this started the ball rolling.

"Hi Ronny, long time no speak, it's -------- how are you"?

"Oh hi, how's you chick"?

"Not so good, me and Brian have had a fight and he said me and the kids have to leave"

"Oh right". "Fuck him". "Just come and stay with me then".

"Come and stay with you"? "Somebody told me you're in love now and going with some blonde lass from Scotland"?

"In love ha ha". "Fuck her too, I'm just shagging her".

"What would she say about your ex-fiancé moving in with you with her kids"?

"Like I said, I'm just shagging her now and fuck her like I said".

"Well Ronny, thanks for the offer and let me think about it".

The first part of the trap was set. She continued to message him over the next few days and kept sending me every single screenshot. One of his exes was getting married in a week to a lovely guy and she started messaging him too.

"Hi Ronny, it's ------- how are you"?

"Oh hiya chick, long time no hear"?
"Yes, well, I was hoping for some advice off you if possible"?

"Of course, anything". "What is it chick"?

"Well, I'm supposed to be getting married next week but I'm having second thoughts".

"Why are you having second thoughts chick"?

"I can't stop thinking about you Ronny and our time together". "Is that wrong of me"?

"No, it's perfectly normal". "Just cancel the wedding and come and stay with me in Carstairs no problem".

"Oh right". "Hopefully you're single right now then"?

"Of course I am". "I heard you were getting married and hoped you'd message me". "I was waiting for this text".

"Oh right, well I'll let him know then and get back to you in a few days".

You can see how this pattern is forming? The daft bastard answered every single text to each of the girls, and I was cringing reading them back. How could my ex-wife fall for this pish? Her mental breakdown the year before all makes sense now. Him messaging her all this utter bullshit too.

We let this continue for a few weeks more and then we had all the evidence that we needed. We got the first Lady to message my ex-wife, and they started up a conversation on social media. The Lady said that she had some information for my ex-wife and if she was ok to send it on.

My ex-wife agreed. Now, this first Lady, I had never met or spoke to her in my life and for Ronny to be engaged to the poor lassie, he never ever mentioned her once to me. That's how I had no clue who she was until she contacted me through a third party.

The first lady had every single screenshot of what all the girls had sent him and that he had sent back and BOOM, the house of love cards came tumbling down in a few short seconds. The first Lady and my ex-wife then traded messages all night long as my ex-wife's world came tumbling down.

She was supposed to meet up with him in a few days for another romantic tryst but after less than 24 hrs she decided to confront him with the damning evidence. Another family ruined and another notch on the bedpost. He didn't give a flying fuck as ever.

Once the dust settled, I asked the first Lady if she was still in contact with my ex-wife to which she replied, "Yes". I asked her if she could forward a message on from myself as that last bit of closure for me. "Sure".

Marie,
**   Both of you daft bastards should've known better than to even try and take me on. Take me on at your peril and you lose royally. If he was a man and contacted me and said that after we had split, if it was ok to fire in there then crack on. There are man's rules and he didn't just cross the line, he ripped the complete cunt oot of it.**

Now, in years to come you will need to explain your actions to our children. Not right now because they are children but when they are adults you will. You haven't just let me down but,

our friends, your own family but most importantly our children down.

Last thing. I promise you this right now. If we never had children together, I would sit back and watch him do to you what he's done to these thirty other women in the group chat I'm in. You can't see it now, but I've actually saved your life here.

It's not just me who has gotten closure today. There's thirty happy women tonight who have got there closure too with this absolute monster. What was it your Social Media header said the other day? It seems to have disappeared for some strange reason….

Now I know what it feels like to be loved, you complete me.

Did he aye…. X

CHAPTER NINE
THE JAZZ SINGER

After all the nonsense of my ex and best man had finally been put to bed. Something else was starting to crop up now. The Scottish girl I was dating was starting to show her true colours. She was in an abusive relationship before dating me so probably thought that speaking to me like she spoke to her ex was pretty normal. Eh, no pal.

I got a very interesting friend request that kinda blew me away. Jennifer the Jazz Singer that sang in the bar I worked in, back in Duquesa. We exchanged a few friendly messages. Nothing spectacular, just asking how each other was etc.

Things were getting worse and worse with Sharon. She came out for my birthday week at the end of March and on her first day here we just decided to call it a day. The distance thing etc just wasn't going to work out. We said we'd have a nice week and when she went back to Scotland then that would be it.

We did have a nice week and to be honest, it was sad to see her go but it had run its course. It was my first dip into the Lady department after my wife, so it was a nice introduction to be honest. A nice woman but it just wasn't to be.

Word got out that I was single and as ever the inbox started to fill up ha ha. One in particular caught my eye though this time and it was Jen, the Jazz Singer.

"I'm sorry to hear about you and Sharon, Scott".

"Och it's fine Jen, thanks for the message".

"I loved the way you always treated her like a Queen". "I know you're probably not ready right now, but I'll be happy to wait for you until you are".

Wait! What? I'm thinking. I had to read that again. Yes, she did type that out.

"Ermmmm, don't you have a boyfriend Jen"?

"No, we split a few weeks ago now". "Look, let me take you away for your birthday". "What do you think"?

"What do I think"? "Ermmmm yaha".

This woman was absolute essence. Yes, I had just split with Sharon, and she had just split with her boyfriend but up until this point, I had never seen or met a more beautiful woman in my life, so the date was set. It was a few days away and I seriously had to pinch myself.

She had booked a five-star hotel for the night to take me away for my birthday and it was genuinely just the most amazing night. I don't know who was more infatuated with who, it was that amazing. This woman was absolutely perfect and up to that point, was everything I ever wanted.

The morning after in the five-star hotel, we went to the restaurant for breakfast. Every single man in the place was looking at Jen, open mouthed at her beauty, but she took no notice of it all whatsoever which I loved. She was so sweet and beautiful.

It was a complete whirlwind for the next month. She'd come to me down in La Linea and I'd go up to hers at the weekend to Marbella. I'd go and watch her sing at whatever venue she was singing at every Friday and Saturday. I was in complete dreamland with my dream girl. Nothing could possibly go wrong. Could it?

We'd go on wee day trips and weekends away. It truly was magical. I couldn't believe that this sweet and sensational human being was even interested in me. I was delighted with the short time that I had with her and didn't want it all to end.

One day she got out of my bed in La Linea and was acting very very strange. I have absolutely no idea why, still to this day, what happened. She went back to Marbella, and I got a message off her saying.

"Look Simon, I'm sorry if you feel hard done by here but I'm ending it".

That was it. Genuinely it. That's how it ended. We had such an amazing month with not one crossed word. Complete infatuation from both sides. Looking back now, it was probably moving far too fast in such a short space of time, but I haven't heard from her once since. Very strange.

By now I had moved out of Nell and Luciano's. I had a friend who worked in the prison service in Gibraltar who had a colleague that was looking for a tenant, so I moved into a six-bedroom Villa with a swimming pool and rented a room.

There were only three other tenants in the Villa at the time. A guy who was the same age as me called Andy and a young lad that worked with Andy called Alfie. They both worked for a gardening and landscape company in Gibraltar and seemed pretty sound.

The other was a young woman from Venezuela named Kelly, but we had hardly seen any of her. She had a broken ankle and was hobbling about the Villa from time to time. She kept herself to herself but would pop out to the pool every now and then and get in to cool off.

Andy was a complete pisshead and was drunk every single day. Alfie had parents up the coast so most weekends he'd go up there. I hadn't really chatted to Kelly as she only spoke Spanish, and I only knew a little of that language then and just said the odd hello.

After getting the message from Jen, I went to the shops and put a crate of Beer in the fridge and went to bed feeling all sorry for myself. I promised myself; I'd just get up the next day and relax beside the pool and sink said crate of beer and get some tanning done.

I got up and made some food and the villa was eerily quiet. I went through to Auld Alan's granny flat next door to ask him if anybody was around. He said that Alfie had went to his parents for the weekend and Andy had gone to Morocco with some friends. "Just you and Kelly I think pal" he said.

I go to the pool after my food and take a couple of cold beers out. I can hear this tapping noise behind me and it's Kelly hobbling towards the pool in her crutches with her bikini on, so I start laughing. She laughs back and says something to me in Spanish. Probably telling me off.

Now I'm 41 at this point. Single and about to get blind drunk beside the pool and there's a stunning 25 year old Venezuelan in her bikini down on her arse trying to get into the pool and I'm pishing myself laughing at her. There are only two sunbeds so when she gets out the pool she gets on the one beside me.

Now, bearing in mind I hadn't really spoke to this woman whatsoever I thought I'd break the ice.

"Cerveza"?

"Si" she replies.

We had a lovely wee day at the pool and communicated the best we could. She was asking about Jen as she'd seen her around the Villa, and I explained in the best Spanish that I knew that we had finished. All of a sudden, she took my hand and put it inside the top of her bikini.

Oh…..

I decided to call it a day. We weren't drunk by any stretch of the imagination however I didn't want things to be confusing as we had to live together. Don't get me wrong she was lovely but at that time, I didn't think it was right thing to do as much as I wanted to.

I was already starting to write my second book "Hugo" by now, so retired to my room after a shower. I got the laptop out and started to type away on that. The last I remember looking at the clock, it was after midnight and suddenly I hear that familiar tapping noise again.

Kelly was on the bottom floor, and I was on the first floor. The tapping noise was Kelly's crutches, and the noise was getting closer and closer until finally my door handle goes down and in she hobbles. She has a pair of skimpy shorts on and small boob tube.

She lifts the boob tube up and takes the shorts off and climbs into my bed. I'm completely stunned.

"This is our little secret ok"? she says

"Ermmm, I thought you didn't speak English"?

She put her finger over my mouth to indicate the shoosh sign and took my laptop and put it on the floor. Now there's only so much a man can resist lads. This became a nightly occurrence for the next three months and it was a very welcome distraction from the departed Jen.

Soon after our little Villa fling, Kelly moved out as her ankle had fully healed and she had gotten a job up in Madrid with some other friends from Venezuela. It was fun and showed me that I hadn't lost it after Jen. It was time to find a proper girlfriend.

I was sick of this dating nonsense and these little flings that had been happening. I joined some dating apps and decided to only swipe right if she blew me away. This went on and on and during this time I had finished writing my second Book "Hugo". I was ready.

I had matched with this stunning blonde Lady named Caroline. We got chatting and she was in the middle of moving house. After a few days it became apparent that moving house was her priority at that time which was fair enough.

She opted to pick things back up when she had settled into her new place. She looked like Holly Willoughby a little bit and seemed posh and classy.

Something I definitely wasn't used to coming from a working-class town on the West Coast of Scotland, where people call a spade a spade.

I didn't really match up nor did anyone really stand out to me until out of the blue a few weeks later I get a message….

CHAPTER TEN
SWEET CAROLINE

"Hi Simon, sorry, that's me all settled in my new place". "I see you are still on this dating app so that's good ha ha". "Let's meet up".

"Oh, I didn't think you'd get back to me Caroline".

"I said I would didn't I"?

"Yes, you did". "Were would you like to meet"?

"Estepona on Sunday at the Port ok"?

"Sounds good". "1pm"?

"See you there mister".

Shit, what is going on here. I've got a date with Holly Willoughby. I spend the next few days sorting my clobber out and getting a haircut and a shave. I earn £1000 a month in Security, and this woman looks seriously high maintenance. Let's just have a laugh on the date and that'll be that.

The Sunday arrives and I get the bus from La Linea up to Estepona and there she is waiting for me at the bus stop. I get off the bus and she looks absolutely sensational. Bright Red lipstick and a lovely blue dress on.

"Hi, I'm Caroline" she says. She sounds like a member of the Royal Family (No joke)

"Oh, hi Caroline, I'm Scott pleased to meet you". Says the NED from Ayrshire….

We walk the short distance to the Port of Estepona and I'm already thinking, what the fuck am I doing here? I'm going out with a cast off from the Royal Family with the accent and everything. The fuck am I going to talk to her about? Polo and the Conservative Party. She better no be a fucking Tory.

We have such an amazing first date and we do what I do best and just get pissed. We go on a pub crawl around the Port. Eat some Food and do some dancing. What a laugh. I thought, one drink and doon the road but that wasn't the case.

The last bus was at 6pm and I didn't want to go but had work in the morning. We head to the Pizza place beside the bus stop to eat before I go.

"Oh, why do you have to go just now Scott"?

"It's the last bus and I have work in the morning".

"Well what time is your work"?

"9am".

"Well, what if you come back to mine and we can have more Wine on the balcony, and I can drive you to the Gibraltar border in the morning"?

"Oh" …. "Ok then, why not".

This was the start of an on and off relationship with Caroline for the next two years or so. We'd split and get back together and so on. It was very difficult for me to please her financially as she always wanted the best of everything and that's what she was used to.

I was making a grand a month and found my gambling spiralling out of control yet again trying to win money to take her to the fancy hotels she wanted to go to so inevitably I'd have to lie about why I couldn't see her that weekend. I had gambled all my wages trying to make her happy.

Caroline had a few issues and I'm not going to blurt them out in a book. She was a lovely human being but just not for me in the end. I haven't got a bad word to say about her and wish her all the best in the future. She did come back into my life though a few times later on in the story….

NOVEMBER 2019

After a few weeks at the Villa, I was in next door talking to Alan and Judith in their wee granny flat for a chin wag.

"Right Scott" says Judith. "There's a girl moving in soon in a few days".

"Right" ..... I say back

"Don't worry, we've warned her about you already ha ha".

"Warned her about me"? "They come to my room in this Villa ha ha".

A few days later myself and auld Alan are heading out for a few beers to a local bar and this young couple are walking towards us. Alan proceeds to tell me that this is the new girl that's moving in that's coming towards us. We do the introductions and head on our way to the bar.

"What do you think then lad"? says Alan

"Didn't really look at her pal to be honest".

That was that really. We stayed out and had a few beers and planned to do the same the night after. I went to bed and got up in the morning and the new girl "Jade" was in the kitchen. She was tall, mid 20's and covered in tattoos. We got talking away and she was sound.

"If you need shown around the local area pal then just let me know" I said. "I can show you where the local supermarkets are and the wee pubs etc ha ha".

"Yeah, that's all I need to know I suppose ha ha" she said back

"In fact, me and Auld Alan are heading out tonight if you fancy a beer or three"?

"I'll see how I feel later, I'll let you know".

Later that early evening Alan calls me from next door to tell me that he has an upset tummy so won't be coming out, so I head down and chap Jade's door.

"Ermmm, this isn't how it looks but Alan had just phoned me to say that he has an upset stomach so won't be coming out for beers". "I'm still heading out for a couple if you want me to show you around a wee bit"?

"Sure, let me get a shower and I'll see you in half an hour".

We head out and have a really good laugh. The guy we saw her with the night before turned out to be her ex-boyfriend and he was helping her move out of the apartment they had shared together. We kissed that night and when I woke up in the morning, she was in my bed and didn't leave it for six months after that.

MARCH 2020 - THE COVID LOCKDOWN

The beauty of the COVID lockdown for me was that I lived in a six-bedroom Villa in Southern Spain with a Pool and a BBQ area and I had my two best pals on the property at that time as well. Auld Alan and Jade. After our first drunken night, me and Jade got on like a house on fire.

There are friends with benefits and then there's best friends with benefits. At that time, she really was my best friend. She made me feel alive again and was so much fun. She was a free spirit like me, and we had so much fun and I didn't want it to end.

The issue I had with her is that she loved attention and sought it in any way that she could. It was

COVID and we were locked down, so it was always going to be difficult for her to get that. I knew that every time we fell out pre-COVID, she would go and fuck other Men.

She wasn't my woman so what could I do? There was a Spanish guy she knew at the end of our street with a Campervan, and she would just go away every time we argued and then come back to me. It's how it was. We both knew when Covid was over, we'd both be off. That was to be the case.

She ended up seeing some boy that was in the Gibraltar Regiment and the last I heard was that they got married and moved back to her native Wales so best of luck to her too. I bear her no ill will. She sent me a message when my dad died and I appreciated that so much. x

JUNE 2020

Spain had decided to let us back out of our homes and myself, and Caroline got back in touch again. I was really concerned for her during COVID as I thought she would really struggle being locked up, but it had the opposite effect on her. She really got into her home workouts etc and seemed a totally different person. Shall I give it another go with her?

We decided we'd at least try. As ever the first few months again were excellent. She did seem like a new person again but then some old traits came back, and it was very clear that although we liked each other very much, we were in completely different lanes career wise.

She liked the finer things in life which was fine. She would never bring herself down to my level and that was an issue for me. I felt comfortable in a room full of millionaires or a room full of working-class people from Council houses. That was Caroline's issue. The latter would be her worst nightmare.

That's the difference right there. I'm a social chameleon and can mix with anybody from any sort of class. We're all the same in my opinion. I could never take her to a rough bar on the West Coast of Scotland and that started to grate on me. How could I take her home?

It wasn't going to be long before I'd get that very call.

CHAPTER ELEVEN
DEVASTATING NEWS FROM HOME

AUGUST 2020

We were all still in the middle of the COVID pandemic. My relationship with Caroline was clinging on by a thread now as well. I had lost my job in Security now due to the pandemic and I was working in recruitment to survive and survive I was barely doing at this point along with everyone else.

I'm in the office one day and I notice on my phone that I have a few missed calls and some from my Mum's friends which is very odd indeed. Suddenly my phone goes again and it's my uncle Colin, so I pick up.

"Hello Colin, how's it going"?

"Here son, your Mum needs to talk to you". "Hawd on a minute". "Tina, it's Simon".

"Hello son, I'm sorry to tell you but your dad died in a car crash this morning". "That's all we know right now". "The Polis are here". "Here's your uncle Colin back".

I couldn't believe my ears. A car crash? No? His little brother died in a car crash that I was in myself. What the fuck is this? Are we cursed? A million thoughts went through my head in a minute. Colin was talking to me, but I couldn't hear a word he was saying. The tears were flooding.

Luckily, I still had Caroline with me at this point, and she helped me out with things. I drove my car up to hers and she dropped me off at the airport to go home a few days later once everything was sorted out in Spain.

I got home around three days or so after he died. I genuinely felt like a spare prick at a wedding at the time. I felt as though everything was already done and sorted before I got there. My relationships with my kids were literally finished and with family members too it was very strained.

It was all very confusing if I was going to see the kids when I was home or not and we had arranged to meet whilst we awaited the funeral arrangements. It was during COVID times, so everything was all very confusing with that too.

We were only allowed twenty people at his graveside due to COVID restrictions, and my Mum had to pick the twenty people. Obviously, some family members had to be left out and my Mum had to be ruthless which she was and I especially, respected her decisions.

The 2-3 weeks I had home were a bit of awakening for me. I had to build bridges not just with my kids but with some family members too and I certainly did that. Well, with the family members anyway. Good and bad.

The meeting with the kids was coming up and we hadn't even buried my dad yet. They arrived from Girvan, and my ex-wife entered the living room first, then my daughter Paige followed by my son Aiden. They had requested one of my sisters and my brother to be there also.

It was the first time I had seen my ex-wife since I had left for Spain nearly two years earlier and I was delighted with how horrific she looked. The children looked amazing, and I hoped that we could leave the room and get back to where we left off and I could be their dad again. It wasn't to be.

From the off it was clear the children had been briefed up with a script by their mother and I got told by both my children later, that this was indeed the case. I was pissing against the wind from the second they entered the room and I sensed how things were going.

I decided to mix it up a little and put the ball in their court.

"I respect both of your decisions here today". "I'll say one last thing". "I'm both of yours Dad and the second that you want or need me back in your lives then I'll be there".

That was it. I stood up and walked out the room. What more could I do or say? One that really irked me through all of this was my family's attitude towards myself through all of the situation with my children. I think the only person I never fell out with over it was my brother.

Even my mother apologised to me recently as my ex-wife always came across as that butter wouldn't melt type of character and if she ever tells you that it's raining outside. Please go outside and double check.

It was devasting for me at the time that my mother took her side. Not now.

My Dad's funeral was the most beautiful day. We told the twenty people who were to be present at the graveside. My Dad actually died of a heart attack at the wheel and crashed the NHS van into a parked car but was already dead before impact.

We requested as he was a NHS worker that if people could, then just to line the route of his funeral cortege on the way to his final resting place to possibly clap him on the way past. What was to follow will stay with me for the rest of my life.

My Dad was a very quiet unassuming guy. The streets were lined for him with people. The Labour Club car park in Saltcoats was packed with people to see him off and even Saltcoats shoreline had people on it. My heart was completely bursting with pride for him.

He got an amazing send off. My children were there but even again at the wake; they were glued to their mother which was fine. I accepted it. At that time, it is what it was. I caught up with the rest of my family members that day and we gave my dad an amazing send off.

How my mother carried herself for those few weeks I was home is something I'll never forget too. We had more flowers in our house than every flower shop in the district combined. Everybody came to see her. The outpouring of love from everyone was absolutely unbelievable.

It was time for me to go back to Spain. This was the first time I really thought about just staying in Scotland and not going back. What did I really have to go back for? A strained relationship and a shite job? I wrote something on my dad's flowers card and told him in the funeral parlour as well.

"I'm coming for it all"!
I got back on that plane back to Spain determined more than ever. I was going to keep that promise to my dad. I had mended the fences I needed to mend that I could and genuinely came back to Spain a new man. Caroline picked me up from the airport and I was going back to hers for a few days to relax. Or so I thought.

As soon as I got back to her apartment the interrogation started.

"So, what happened with your children"? "What happened with this"? "What happened with that"?

"Caroline, I'm physically and mentally exhausted". "I've genuinely just had the worst two weeks of my life". "Please let me rest tonight and we can talk tomorrow".

"No, we can talk now". "I deserve to know". "I'm your partner so tell me".

No joke, this shit went on for hours and hours and hours. She wouldn't let it stop. Eventually she falls asleep, yes, she falls asleep. I'm now awake. Completely exhausted listening to her snoring away. Aye nae bother. The next day was the same. Something happened when I was back home as well.

Two junkies were fighting over money at a cashpoint at ASDAs in Ardrossan as me and my Uncle Colin were stopping for some Beers and I thought it was quite funny. Just normal for where we're from and I pointed them out to Colin.

We got back to Colin's house and his partner "Sandra" was there and I proceeded to tell her about the two junkies fighting over the money at the cashpoint and I said to her, "Thank God Caroline didn't come and see that".

Sandra says "How"?

"Well, she's probably never seen anything like that before and would probably be scared ha ha".

"Well whit are you way her fur then"? "This is who you are and where you come from". "If she doesn't like that then tell her to get tae fuck".

I thought, do you what Sandra, you're right. I took two more days of her shite constantly looking for an argument when all I probably needed was a bit of love and tenderness and finally told her to get to fuck. Luckily my car was there so I just got into it and drove back to the Villa. I'd had enough.

I came back to Spain a new man and wasn't putting up with her shite for one more single second. I had to move on. I promised my Dad I was coming for it all and that's what I was going to do.

I ended up getting out of that recruitment job rapid and got some good security work again and things were starting to look up again. I started writing another book again and felt inspired. Life events sometimes give you that massive kick up the arse that you need.

You start to realise what's important in life and what's not. It wasn't just to do with work, books, writing and a good lady. I wanted it all but the thing I wanted the most was my babies back in my life. I didn't know how or when it was going to happen, but I knew that it would.

CHAPTER TWELVE

IVAN DRAGO

I sign up for the dating apps once more for some window shopping….

I scroll for a month or two and absolutely nothing catches my eye. I see Caroline on them all and quickly swipe left. As nice a person as she is there was just no way. We had tried for a second time and it's a no.

I come across this absolutely beautiful woman. Anna, 25 years old. Ukrainian, tall, dark hair and the most beautiful woman I'd ever seen. I thought, I'll swipe right but absolutely no chance is she swiping right on me.

I had completely forgotten all about her and a few days later I got a notification. You have matched with Anna. I'm thinking, Anna? I open my phone and click on the notification and there she is. The Ukrainian goddess. I'm thinking I'm being set up here. How wrong could I be….

OCTOBER 2020

After a few weeks of talking to Anna. We decide to meet in Algeciras. She had moved there from the Ukraine with her three-year-old son to escape her abusive junkie ex-boyfriend. I meet her in a local park, and we decide to go for Coffee.

She was so beautiful. Big lips, a perfect big white smile. Beautiful mysterious eyes. Tall and so shy as well which I liked. She was a woman that only I could dream of. She was utter perfection.

She doesn't speak a word of English or Spanish as she's just moved here and she's very shy too. My Russian and Ukrainian wasn't really up to speed so we did the best we could through Google translate and all seemed to be going well. Afterwards we set up another date and shortly afterwards, she became girlfriend number two of my Spanish adventure after Caroline.

Her living conditions were terrible. Her mother had married an older Spanish guy, and they lived in a shitty little three-bedroom apartment. Anna sleeping on the floor of a small bedroom so her son could sleep in the bed. Her thirteen-year-old sister in another room and her mum and stepdad in another.

As the months rolled on, I was getting more and more frustrated with the stuff she was telling me as her English got much better about her Mum. I was slowly but surely beginning to detest the woman. She treated Anna like shit and Anna was such a beautiful soul and just took it.

I was getting more and more frustrated at the Villa by now as well. My time there was almost up. They were letting anybody that could pay the rent move in and the guy that replaced Jade in her room really got on my tits, so I felt like it was time to move out.

Anna was in cramped conditions, and I needed a new place, so it made sense for us to get our own place so that's what we did. She said that her Mum knew a place close by to hers that would be perfect for us. Little did I know that it was straight across the fucking corridor, from her Mums door.

We went with it and by April 2021 we had moved in together to our first flat straight across from her mother's. Biiiiiiiiiiiiiiig mistake. At first it was fine obviously but her mother still thought it would be ok to rip the complete piss out of her whenever she wanted to. Eh, no pal.

It caused argument after argument. This woman would not lift a finger in her own apartment and expect Anna to do everything for her. Cook and clean. Everything basically. She wasn't on as far as I was concerned and I made my feelings known. Again, it led to another break up.

I think the issue with Anna was that she was very young and just ran away from her problems instead of facing them head on. This is why she is constantly running away from everything in life. I hope that she would be mature enough to sort our small issues out, but it wasn't to be.

I think we'd been in the apartment around a month, and a half and she was dragging her stuff back across the corridor to the house of horrors. Go! No problem. If you really want to go back to her then please be my guest. She was gone and I never heard another peep from her again. Until….

JUNE 2021

I'm back on the dating apps yet again and see that Caroline is still on there. I thought, fuck it, let's swipe right for a laugh and see what happens.

"Congratulations, you have matched with Caroline"!

I thought ha ha, here we go again. We start chatting and she was like, "Oh no, what a nightmare". "Why don't I buy some Mexican Food and bring cocktails down to cheer you up"?

I thought, do you know what? Fuck it. Anna walked past my door for nearly a month now and hadn't been an adult, chapped it and asked to talk so fuck it. "Aye, you do that and come down".

Caroline comes down to the apartment I shared with Anna and texts me to let me know that she's outside. I was on the top floor. The fourth floor, so went downstairs to help her as I knew she would have a few bags. I hadn't seen her for a year either so was looking forward to seeing her again.

I went downstairs and she got out the car. I gave her the auld Spanish, kiss on two cheeks thing. Took the bags off her and proceeded up the stairs. I can hear people coming down the stairs. It's only Anna's Mum, stepdad, Sister and Son. Fuuuuuuuuuuuuuck. Thankfully no Anna.

However, I knew she'd know in two minutes flat. I'm absolutely shitting my pants thinking big Ivan Drago is going to boot my door off the hinges and fling me and Holly Willoughby aboot Algeciras but as the alcohol started flowing, I was thinking, what's this got to do with her? Fuck it.

Caroline then went to bed as she had work in the morning and I stayed up and had a one-man party then crashed on the couch. I woke Caroline up in the morning and walked her down the stairs and out to her car. She wanted to try again. I said I'd think about it and off she went.

I started to walk back up the stairs and Anna's Mum's dog was coming down the stairs like it had got out the apartment. I'm like, "Lucky, how did you get out"? "Let's get you home pal". I start going up and up the floors and who's stood outside my front door arms folded? Yuuuup. Oor Drago.

"What was that bitch doing here"?

Fucking hell I'm thinking.

"Ermmmm, I haven't heard from or spoke to for over a month Anna". "You walk past my door daily". "You can't fucking knock it and talk like an adult no"?

"I was coming back from the Gym last night". "I turned the corner and saw you kissing her on the cheeks and helping her upstairs with bags".

"Ah, that's why I passed the rest of your family and not you on the stairs then"?

"I could hear that bitch laughing and giggling all night, and I wanted to boot that door down".

"Funny you should say that" ….

"Can we talk Scott"?

"Oh, now you want to talk huh"?

Now I was in a fucking position. I was in a love triangle that a day ago I wasn't in. I must choose between my first girlfriend in Spain or the second one. I had no intention of ever getting back with Caroline but what about giving Anna another go?

I think Anna just didn't want to lose out to Caroline and vice versa. I knew I'd lose the other one forever if I'd make a choice. I chose Anna and decided to break the news to Caroline who obviously wasn't happy. Again after a few months, things fizzled out with Anna due to her Mum.

On the August I got invited to a friend's pool party in Santa Margarita. They lived in a beautiful, enclosed Villa with a stunning pool. Halfway through the party I got chatting to one of the hosts "Steve" and he asked me if I knew anybody as they were looking for a lodger.

I asked him how much they were looking for and it was literally half of what I was paying for a shitty apartment with all bills included or stay in that flat directly across from Anna's Mum. It was a sign and my chance to get out of dodge. I could move in, in the next fortnight. Delighted.

It was like rehab for me moving in with Paul and Steve. They had such a nice tranquil Villa in the middle of nowhere with a pool. I got right back into my training again and was able to just relax in peace beside the pool on my days off.

The beauty of staying there was that I took a six-month sabbatical from alcohol as well and got myself really fit and strong again but as ever, it doesn't last, and I just got right back to ripping the absolute hole out of it as ever once I get started again.

CHAPTER THIRTEEN
HAS JJ MET HIS TERESA?

I finally put the nightmare of oor Drago and Algeciras behind me and move in with my friends Paul and Steve. They have this amazing 3 bedroom Villa with a Pool and a granny flat out the back, where Paul's Mum "Trish" lives. They also have a foster son named "Sean" who lives there too.

Life is really going great again. I'm working away in Security still and have an interview for a job in the Gaming industry in Gibraltar. The gaming industry is basically the gambling industry there. I have two interviews actually, in two separate departments of the same company on the same day.

I go for the job interviews and they both seem to go well. Later, that evening I get a call from the HR department saying that I have been accepted for both and I have to choose. I find out nearly 4 years down the line now that I've made the right one.

I give my notice for the Security job, and I can now look forward to my new one.

OCTOBER 2021

It had been a few months now since I had split up from Anna and I was starting to feel a bit lonely again. I had been tanning well over the summer and hitting the Gym hard, so I was looking decent. I had got myself a new job and was starting that next month too. It was time to start dating again.

I had matched with this blonde woman about twenty minutes up the coast. She was Irish and her name was Helen. She looked great. She looked fun and her social life looked good too. We arranged a date halfway between both of us for drinks and Tapas.

We go on the date, and we have a right good laugh. She asks me about myself, and I proceed to tell her about my books etc, especially "The Bunnet". After proceeding to tell her what it's all about she asks me if I'm taking the piss?

I'm like "What do you mean am I taking the piss"?

"Ermm, you're Scottish and I'm Irish".

"Riiiiiiiiiight", I reply

"The town JJ & Teresa meet in is called Ballincollig"?

"Riiiiiiiiiight", I reply

"That bar "Healy's" that they all drank in"? "In Ballincollig"?

"Yeeeeeeeeeeeees"?

"My Grandad drank in there". "His wake after his funeral was in there and that's where we used to go for our school holidays".

"Na man"? I say in complete and utter disbelief.

So, three years previously I had written a book about a Scottish guy that goes to Ireland meets this buxom Irish lassie? The guy was loosely based on myself. The girls sounds exactly like Helen and then she proceeds to tell me all of this? Madness, absolute madness.

The date ends and we hastily arrange another. I can't believe what she's just told me. Has JJ met his Teresa? I got back to Paul and Steve's and tell them right away. I then put it on all of my Socials, and my friends and family can't believe it either. Mental.

After a few dates, myself and Helen decide to give it a go. She lives up in Sabinillas, the wee town next to the Port of Duquesa where my Spanish adventure had started. I had come full circle. I basically moved in with her right away and kept paying my rent at Paul and Steve's just in case.

It started off great as most relationships do. She was a beauty therapist and had her own business and I had now started my job in the Gaming industry. There was a big Irish community there and the hub of the community was a local Irish bar which was everyone's second home.

A few patterns started to emerge that I wasn't happy with. The woman that I had met was so confident and outgoing and very popular in the community. Unfortunately, that wasn't the same person when we got home. She acted like a five-year-old behind closed doors and she just wasn't for me.

She would constantly tell me about guys messaging her. Men adding her on all of her socials but not to worry as she wasn't accepting them. She was keeping her married name too and showed no signs of getting a divorce. All very odd behaviour so after around 10 months or so.

I decided to call it a day. It just wasn't working for me. It was a shame really as I actually saw myself marrying Helen. She was the person that I could see myself growing old with. There were so many things I liked about her but inevitably in the end, too many things I didn't.

I contacted Paul and Steve again and asked if I could move back into the Villa and they said no problem. I had stopped paying my rent a few months previously as I decided to move in with Helen permanently. Thankfully they said yes so it was back to the Villa once more.

I was kinda sick of everything again. I just locked myself away and started on another book. Done my training and my tanning again as ever and sort of locked myself away from the World again. I just didn't want to know.

During this period my daughter Paige had got back in touch with me and had asked if I meant what I said at my dad's funeral about wanting her in my life.

"Of course I do darling" was my reply.

We began talking again and I was completely elated. She was nearly 16 now so wasn't stupid and was starting to see everything from both sides. Her Mum's and her dad's now and was starting to very quickly make her own mind up on things which was great.

She even came out to Spain with my Mum to visit and we really connected again which was amazing. We talked about everything when she became an adult, and I did nothing but tell her the truth. I told her everything.

I didn't blame her Mum for leaving me at all. It's how her and the best man from our wedding did it. There was absolutely no need for that at all so that's why I got the both of them back a belter.

I wasn't the greatest husband in the World no. I was very popular with the Ladies when I was younger. I played on and acted on that multiple times so completely deserved my wife to go. She was fully aware of everything and stayed.

I remember a friend saying to me once.

"Your wife could walk into the bedroom and catch you with three wimmin in bed with you and she'd just ask them to leave and then get back to normal again".

He was right. I knew that and all of my friends knew that, and probably up until I was around thirty, I genuinely didn't care. I was in a loveless marriage from day one really and I never should have done it but hey ho. We live and learn.

I also went for a long weekend with my daughter, her boyfriend and my Mum to Liverpool as well. I had been cast in a Movie amazingly and I went there to meet the cast which was an amazing experience. My daughter is a big Beatles fan too so the full experience and to spend time with her was great.

I was starting to get itchy feet again and was looking for some female company so signed up yet again to the dating apps.

Posh Caroline was on there. Helen was back on them too and guess who else I seen on there? Oor Drago. I always felt as though there was unfinished business there with Anna. I knew that I could date Caroline again too if I wanted to, but Anna is the one I was drawn to so swiped right on her. Again.

I had totally forgot all about that I swiped right on her and in work about a month later at around 2am on a Sunday morning I get a notification on my phone from Tinder.

You have matched with Anna!!

I didn't think much off and didn't even open my phone up for a look or anything and then two minutes later.

Anna has sent you a message!!

I open my phone and to my astonishment it was her. I genuinely had forgot that I had swiped right on her a month previously and there it was. A message from my beautiful ex Ukrainian girlfriend.

"I can't believe"!! she had messaged me

We start texting again and agree to meet up that weekend. I really did miss her, and she ticked so many boxes for me. I had to give her one last chance. She is a special human being. Hopefully the seventeen-year age gap doesn't become an issue this time.

I guess we'll soon find out.

CHAPTER FOURTEEN
ROUND TWO DRAGO?

Oor Drago and I decided to go for round two and give it another go. I was fascinated that this beautiful, young and tall beauty would be even interested in me, but she was. She was infatuated and I loved that.

We started to date again in secret as myself and her mother really didn't get on and she was obviously still living there so we kept it secret for months.

We got on great despite the 17-year age gap between us. She was fun and silly, and I liked that. It's difficult to get a woman my age that is fun and fun she was. She was not only fun but ticked every single box.

After a few months, the cat got out the bag. Her Mum was starting to ask lots of questions. Her younger sister had already guessed who it was that she was seeing. It was finally time to tell her Mum. As you can imagine, it didn't go down well.

Anna was basically forced out of the home, along with her now, five-year-old son and had to stay with a Ukrainian friend of hers in a one bedroomed flat close by to her son's school.

She was sleeping on a sofa bed in the living room of her friend's apartment and yet again, I felt so bad for her and her son. I was living in a luxury Villa with a pool and here these two were in these conditions. Yet again, I felt like I had to act.

I loved Anna, I really did. She is such a beautiful human being who had such a tough life. I wanted to give her the best in life, so I started to look for accommodation yet again for us. I found an amazing three-bedroom flat in La Linea next to Gibraltar.

I told Paul and Steve that I was going to be moving out of the Villa and we got all our stuff together and decided to start another new life together.

FEBRUARY 2023

At the beginning, everything was great of course. She was so house proud and never had a Mop out of her hand. The apartment just stunk of disinfectant constantly. She was forever cleaning, and I didn't mind that.

We were a 45-minute bus journey away from her son's school in Algeciras and Anna also worked full time. I worked nights as well, so it was difficult to see each other.

After a few months of literally not seeing each other and Anna in bed by herself five nights a week, it really did start to fizzle out very very quickly. The final nail in the coffin was not being able to get her son enrolled in a local school so another year at least of this routine just wasn't going to work.

One day, she came home exhausted yet again from another long day working and travelling and basically asked me if I was happy as she wasn't either. I told her that I wasn't too, so we decided to call it a day.

Over the next couple of days her stepdad and Mother came for all of her stuff and here I was back to square one yet again. In a three-bedroom apartment. Views of Morocco and Gibraltar but all on my lonesome once again.

After a month or so I was scrolling through my social media and caught a glimpse of this stunning blonde woman in America. I hadn't spoken to her before or even noticed her. We struck up a conversation and within a month she had booked flights to come and visit me from Detroit.

JULY 2023 – TEAM AMERICA

I go to Malaga airport to pick Carrie up. Again, I'm thinking this is a joke. Ex Playboy Model and stunning. Seems a good laugh and up for a good time. What can possibly go wrong?

Well, it turns out that she's the most annoying woman on the planet with one of those American accents that just go right through you. She's booked up for two weeks as well, but we make the most of it.

It turns out to be a not too bad two weeks really. It's nice to have a stunning woman round the apartment again and it was nice to get out and about with her as well really. As much as she annoyed me, it was pretty sad when she left. I was back on my own again.

For the next two years. I didn't really date many Ladies to be honest. I really missed Anna. It's the one relationship out of them all that hit me the hardest really. I thought about her every single day for the next two years really.

It didn't help that when I looked out of my window, I could see the town that she moved back to just five miles away across the water. I just couldn't connect with her son. God forgive me for saying that but it's simply the truth.

I think if she was on her own then we'd 100% still be together today. We let each other go basically as it wasn't our time. Will it be our time again in the future one day? Who knows.

I felt really bad that I was taking her son out to get his hair cut. Taking her son out to get clothes. Watching the Football, the Wrestling and the Boxing with her son and quite honestly, he wasn't my son.

It had been five years now that my son hadn't wished to speak to me. Again, I get it. The kids get brainwashed by the parent that they live with, but he was now fifteen and I craved to have him back in my life.

What had happened to that special wee guy that I remember? I had a relationship with my daughter now but not my son yet. She had been telling me things as had my Mum, and it wasn't good.

I'd been hearing about him smoking, drinking and even taking drugs. I'd also heard that my ex-wife was just leaving him to his own devices as she had shacked up with a sixty-year-old man twenty miles away from where my son was and didn't want to know.

The stories were getting worse and worse. Then in October of 2023 I'm on a LIVE Podcast on YouTube on a Friday night. I'll never forget it. It was around 11pm over here in Spain and I get a phone call from my mother.

OCTOBER 2023

"Eh hello, it's your Mother and I have your son here".

"Ermmmm, ok", I reply.

"Your ex- Father-in-Law, Mother-in-Law and Sister-in-Law are here with him and they are at the end of their tether with him". "Do you want me to book a flight for tomorrow and bring him out to you in Spain"?

Now, obviously I haven't spoken to my son for five years and the last I seen of him was the week of my father's funeral but without hesitation my mother got a two-word answer straight away.

"Let's go"!!

My Mother booked the flights, booked on their bags and it looked very likely that the very next day, my son and Mother was going to arrive from Scotland. What the actual fuck is going on?

If it had been a few months earlier, my fifteen-year-old son would've had a five-year-old stepbrother and a twenty-eight-year-old step Mother here. Just another mad situation in my life to handle.

My Mother phones the next day to tell me that there's a problem. Aiden has less than six months on his passport so he can't fly. He stays at my Mum's whilst we sort the nightmare of his passport out. In fact, "nightmare" isn't the word.

As much as my Mum is a beautiful soul and a no-nonsense individual. I'd say spelling and Admin are not really her specialist subjects so imagine her trying to sort out my son's passport over the next few days?

I think I spoke to the Woman in the shop from Spain more than my Mum did, stood right next to her in the shop in Saltcoats. Eventually, we think we've got it all done and it gets sent away.

After six weeks or so there's a major fuck up with it and I eventually need to come back to Scotland to sort it all at the major Passport place in Glasgow. The beauty of this is that it's Christmas time. I hadn't spent Christmas Day at my Mum's house for over twenty-five years, so it was absolutely lovely to get that time with my family.

We make a wee trip or two up to Glasgow and eventually we get everything sorted out. They tell us it will be a few days after the New Year, so I book our flights back to Spain.

I spend the next few days or so trying to get to know my son again after all these years and I can tell that he's not the boy I left behind for sure. The manners and the respect had gone. He was a cheeky wee boy, but I had to be patient with him. Who was I to tell him off? It was going to be a long hard road.

The time had come, and we said our farewells. My uncle Colin picked us up and we head for Prestwick Airport. The very same scene from where my ex-wife dropped me with my children at all those years previously.

My Son was coming back with me to start a new life. He had the best opportunity anyone in my family has ever had at fifteen years old. The world at his feet and a brand-new start at life in Sunny Spain.

But will he take it?

CHAPTER FIFTEEN
SPAIN ISN'T FOR YOU SON

We arrive in Spain at Malaga airport. I'm having a fling with a reality TV star from Finland by this point. She lives close by to the airport in Fuengirola, so I dropped my car off with her on the way up and she picked us up.

I need to drop her off in Fuengirola on the way down, so we decide to stop off on the way down for a Beer as well and she gets to meet my son. Tia is only twenty-seven years old and my son is fifteen so it was probably a wee bit awkward for both but they got on very well thankfully.

Tia was covered in tattoos and like to smoke weed so as we get to the bar, she rolls a spliff as I order the drinks. As she's toking away, she asks my son if he wants a toke as he'd already had a cigarette off her.

I decided to try and be the relaxed and cool dad at this point to try and help him settle into life in Spain. I knew that he had been smoking, drinking and taking drugs as well in Scotland so I was completely daft. I wasn't much different at his age so let him have a couple of puffs on it.

We say our farewells to Tia and head down the coast home. I remember the rain that night. I hadn't seen anything like it trying to get home. We eventually get there, and the boy settles into his new surroundings.

He looks like Mowgli out of the Jungle Book the poor boy. His hair is all over the place and he doesn't have many clothes. Yes, I'm partly to blame for that for sure and accept that but I can't believe that he's just been abandoned so much and I'm his last option now really.

I would class myself as quite a smart dresser and I like to be well groomed. I decided that I was going to try and make him into a mini me. We get his hair sorted and start to buy him new clothes and trainers etc.

Now obviously the Spanish style of clothes and trainers is much different to what he was used to but surely, we could get him some better clobber than black trainers and black tracksuit bottoms? I get it, most fifteen-year-old kids in Scotland wear the same get up and he wasn't any different.

I could see that he was turning his nose up to what I was buying him and what I was trying to do for him. He was a bag of bones as well, so I tried my best to feed him up and I also started to take him to the Gym with me to build him up as well.

We went on day trips, weekends away. Trips into Gibraltar to meet Scottish friends of mine. I tried to buy him what he wanted when he wanted it. I tried to teach him how to cook, clean and basically look after himself as he was going to be a man soon.

All the kid wanted to do really was lock himself away in his dark bedroom and stay up all night shouting and bawling with his friends on his PlayStation head set and after a few days or so. That was really starting to get on my tits.

The kid didn't have any respect for me or the very quiet block of apartments that I lived in and very quickly I could see why absolutely everyone in his life has turned their backs on him. I did what I could but inevitably the kid didn't want to be in Spain.

He arrived with me in the January and by the time his sixteenth birthday came in August, I had had enough of his disrespect really. It got to a point where I'd need to take the internet box to work with me at night as his shouting online with his friends was that loud.

I was dating a couple of girls at this point, and it was basically impossible with a fifteen-year-old boy in my apartment as well. He wasn't happy that I was bringing Ladies home and Ladies between twenty-five and thirty aren't looking to adopt a tearaway teenager who has no respect for anyone.

When he moved into his bedroom in the January, everything was brand new. The furniture and the walls were immaculate. By the time he had turned sixteen in the August the walls were Black with his dirty feet constantly up on the walls chatting to his mates, not giving one fuck.

We needed the chat!!

I summoned him to the living room not long after his sixteenth birthday. I had already spoken to his sister Paige about him returning to Scotland and she was willing to allow him to live with her. He came into the living the room.

"You don't want to be here do you"?

"Ermmmm, no, no really".

"Ok son, I'll book you a flight back to Scotland".
"Spain isn't for you son".

I had visions of him staying here. Him coming to the Gym with his auld Da. Us becoming best pals. I had him a job all good to go and it wouldn't have been long before he had made friends working in the bar job I had got him in Gibraltar.

The visions I had for him and me basically turned into a nightmare. All of the stuff that I had heard about him was right. I was gutted really as he had the chance of an absolute lifetime and failed to grasp it. This was his sliding doors moment in life and at 16, he chose to go back to Scotland.

The day came for him to leave, and I drove him up to Malaga airport. I was happy for him that he was going back to where he wanted to be, but I was also angry with him too that he never truly gave life over here a go.

It wasn't long before he wasn't living my daughter Paige over in Scotland and he went to live my estranged sister for a small time too. He then contacted me asking me for money and sent me such a shitty message that we haven't spoken since.

Two weeks after he sent me the shitty message, I get that sliding doors moment call. After he went back to Scotland, he got his seventeen-year-old girlfriend pregnant. At sixteen, my son finds out that he is going to be a father. No job, no prospects and no respect for any human being on the planet.

He could've and should've been chilling in Spain with his dad but now due to his absolute disrespect to everyone on both sides of his family, he now faces the daunting task of raising a child when he can't even look after himself.

It's of course a relationship that I hope to rekindle one day but at this moment in time the relationship is pretty much dead in the water. When he becomes a man, which will be very shortly, he will realise that two word answer I gave to my Mum when he needed me the most. "Let's go"!!

Yes, he will need me now more than ever. Just the same as he will need both families. I never spoke to my parents once in my life the way he decided to speak to me over a phone messenger app. He will learn the very hard way for now and receive some tough love that he needs.

I sincerely hope that he comes out the other end of this. I put on my dad's card on his flowers at his grave that I was coming for it all and I meant that. I've tried to do that since I've had breath in my body, and I hope for the same for my son and soon to be grandson.

I told him when he came to Spain that I didn't want him to fail. I told him that everyone expects him to fail and that he'll be back on a flight to Scotland shortly. Little did I know that this would be the case. I don't see any fight or spirit in him, and I hope that will change now,

He's about to get the biggest wakeup call that we all get. When that tiny little human being gets put into your arms for that first time and they rely on you solely, it's such a weird feeling. You look into their helpless little eyes and make a promise to do the best that you can.

I made that same promise to not just my daughter but my son too. The marriage break-up and all the lies the children were told about me certainly worked for a few years. I managed to repair my relationship with my daughter, but my son is going to be a tougher nut to crack now.

I believe that him and his girlfriend are having a boy as well so hopefully when my Grandson arrives, this might open my son's eyes a little more about what life is really about.

I had a love/hate relationship with my own Dad over the years. I always appreciated what he done for us. He was a functioning alcoholic but taught me so much. He had a work ethic that was second to none. He was quiet and unassuming guy but came alive when he had a drink.

He didn't bother anyone in life and didn't really stand out. His life was his jobs and his family and that was the type of guy he was. Barring my work ethic, I'm nothing really like my own Dad.

I kinda hoped that my boy would be like me, but he isn't either. I left a really nice and well-mannered boy in Scotland at ten years old and to see him so different only five years later is hard to take. I hope that he manages to sort his life out and becomes a great father like my dad.

It's something that will always grate me now until my dying days that up until I left Scotland, it was my favourite thing in the world being a dad. I loved it. It was ripped away from me and I'll probably forever have that part of my soul missing now,

Will I get the opportunity to be a grandfather now? Who knows. There's lots of fences that need to be mended yet again and for the past eight years now, that's all I seem to have been doing.

I spoke to my Mum recently and people keep asking me when I'm coming home to visit. I've severely lost the motivation to come home now and that's so sad. Nobody bothers with me really so why should I? The next year or so is going to be very interesting indeed…..

CHAPTER SIXTEEN
GLENN CLOSE

JULY 2025

The last year since my son left has been quiet really. I've been keeping myself to myself. Keeping busy with my training and my tanning. I had quite a bad accident in February when I fell off my electric scooter so couldn't really train from the February until the June again.

I start to hit the beach clubs as the Summer comes in and I meet a nice Romanian girl one day. Her name is Daga. She tells me that she likes to read books etc, so I tell her that I'm Writer. I tell her that I'll order my first two Books for her and she can read them whilst she's at the beach.

I get a notification that they have arrived at a local Amazon pick up point. A Hostal in my local town. I thought this was very weird but went with it. I went to work as ever at night and decided at 8am when I was finished, I would just pop to the pickup point and collect them for Daga.

I finish work and jump on my electric scooter. I head over the border from Gibraltar into Spain and head to the Hostal. As I'm locking my electric scooter up outside the Hostal, I see this stunning blonde coming towards with a takeaway cup of Coffee in her hand and she looks at me and gives me a huge smile.

I don't think anything of it and head into the Hostal. She stood out like a sore thumb as she had blonde hair, a fair complexion and was absolutely stunning. All very odd for the very South of Spain. I ask the man behind the counter for my packages and receive them. I turn round and who's stood right beside inside the Hostal? The beautiful blonde.

"Hey, you ok"? I ask, just being polite.

"Ermmm, not really" she replies whilst looking sad and down to the floor.
"What's the matter"? I ask

"Well, I need to be out of here by twelve o'clock" she says. "They're kicking me out". "I don't have any money, and I have all of my stuff". "I just arrived here, and I don't know anyone". "I don't know what to do" she says

"Shit". "Ok" I say. "Let's think". "Ok, I've literally just finished my nightshift". "I'll give you my number". "I'll come and meet you later for a Coffee". "I have lots of friends here and I'm sure we'll be able to get you sorted out so don't worry ok"?

"Ok" she says.

I give her my number and head home to shower and get to bed. I wake up in the afternoon and totally forget all about the meeting with the blonde in the morning. I make food and Coffee and chill on my couch for a wee while before starting to sort myself for work again that night.

My phone rings from an unknown number. Now, normally I don't pick up those numbers and I wish I never now but on this occasion I did.

"Hello" I say

"Hi Simon, it's Alina from this morning at the Hostal".

"Oh yes, you ok"?

"You said you would come and meet me"? "They want me to move my stuff out the Hostal".

"Oh yes ok". "Let me shower and I can be there in thirty minutes". "I can whizz round in my Electric Scooter no problem as you're five minutes away".

"Thank you Simon".

I get in the shower and head round to the Hostal. Alina is outside waiting.

"Ok Alina let's go and get a Coffee and I'll make some calls to pals that have Villa's and apartments, and stuff and we'll see what we can do for you".

"I can't leave here because of all my stuff". "They want it moved".

"Stuff"? "How much stuff do you have ha ha"? "Let me go and talk to them, it'll be fine".

I walk in and she shows me her stuff. She literally has fifty suitcases and bags in total stacked all the way along this corridor. No wonder they want her fucking stuff gone. Holy shit.

"Ermmmm, Alina". "Ok, don't lie to me here". "What the fuck is going on"? I ask

"I came down yesterday from Malaga in a Taxi with my stuff and stayed here last night and today they want me to go".

"You came here with all this stuff"?

"Yes, to start a new life" she says

"Holy fuck" I reply. "Ok, so you have no money"? "Nowhere to go"? "You don't know anybody here and there's nowhere to put this stuff"?

"My family will send me money, and they said that they will sort a storage room out for me here over the next couple of days".

"Ok, we need a quick fix for now". "Ok, I need to go to work in a few hours". "I'm trusting you here ok"? "I'll go and get my car". "You can store your stuff in my apartment for a few days until you get sorted with a storge room and money from your family". "You will at least be safe at my apartment".

"Are you sure Simon"?

"I don't see like I have little choice here". "You're lucky that you bumped into me today". "Let's get you sorted out".

I go home on my Electric scooter and leave Alina at the Hostal. I get there and start to pack my car up with her bags and suitcases. It becomes apparent it's going to be two trips, so we get a Taxi to follow me with the rest. I get her and her stuff into my apartment and make her some food.

I try my best to get as much information out of her as possible. She either is a poor soul or the best actress in the World. I need to go to work soon and leave this complete stranger in my apartment. What am I doing I ask myself.

I go to work and tell my colleagues what has happened.

"Are you fucking mad"? One of my colleagues say. "You know she can change the locks tonight and invite whoever there and under Spanish law there's absolutely fuck all you can do now to kick her out"?

Now I'm starting to shit myself. No good deed goes unpunished, so for the rest of the night now, I'm wondering if I'm even going to get back into my apartment in the morning just for doing a good deed. I finish work and head home. I put the key in the door and luckily it turns and opens. I walk inside and Alina is up already and relaxing on the couch.

It was my last shift there so at least I have four days now to get to know her. To give her time now to get money from family or friends. To find her what her story is and to get all of her stuff out of my apartment.

I give her a full double room to herself with two single beds in it and it's stacked from top to bottom with all of her bags. Literally. You can't swing a cat, so I offer her another bedroom to sleep in as the room she in is crammed but she's happy in there.

It becomes very apparent over the next four days that I'm off, that she has pretty bad mental health issues. A very intelligent woman that can speak six different languages fluently, very beautiful, but a few sandwiches short of a picnic. The lights are on, but nobody is home.

The days turn into a week. The week turns into a month and then the month turns into three months. She's thirty-seven years old and can't even make a cup of coffee for herself. I had three months of her constantly waking me up because she was hungry etc as she could do nothing.

I was paying to get her hair done. Her eyes and her nails done. Clothing. I was feeding her, cleaning for her, doing her washing for and taking her out when I was off work. She was becoming more and more in love with me, and the writing was on the wall. I had had enough and wanted her to leave.

I decided to ask her to leave, and I think that she thought I was kidding. I decided on one Tuesday night. Tuesday the 16th of September 2025 that she would be leaving the apartment in the morning. I had had enough of her lies, her bullshit and basically doing absolutely everything for her. The Wednesday morning arrives, and I knock on her bedroom door,

"Alina it's 9am". "You have an hour to get something sorted and I want you out of this apartment today as I told you last night". "Start phoning your family and friends". "If you need a lift or a Taxi somewhere then I'll get that sorted for you but today, you are gone".

As you can imagine this didn't go down well. She wouldn't go. I had some friends come round to try and reason with her also. Again, she refused to leave. I even had to phone Police and again, they came and could do nothing as she was basically living here, and Spanish Law is different.

I was literally stuck with her now and there was nothing I could do. The Spanish Police told me that I had to give her two days to find somewhere to go so I did. I decided to leave and stay with friends and leave this nutter in my house.

I spoke with my Spanish Lawyer and my Landlord too. What a commotion all for doing a good deed for this woman three months previously. Her lies and her false promises had all come to this. I decide to leave and head to my friend's house and whilst I thought this would be the end of it. This day was only just getting started.

Hell, hath no fury like a woman scorned……

CHAPTER SEVENTEEN
BANGED UP ABROAD

I head to my friend's house and after an hour or so I realise that I've left my man bag in the apartment with all my documents in there that I need. My passport and bank cards etc. I head there with a female friend in her 70's as a witness in case Alina says or does anything.

I arrange to stay with friends for a couple of nights too, so I decide to pick up a few things whilst I'm there as well. My friends that I'm staying with aren't home until after 8pm so my plan is to chill with Alan and Judith for the day at their place until I need to go to Paul and Steve's place. The lads in the Villa that I lived with before.

I head to the apartment with Judith and collect a few things. Alina doesn't say a word really. The only thing I ask her for is the spare keys for the apartment which she says that she doesn't have. I know for a fact that she does so now we have another issue.

I head back to Alan and Judith's with Judith and start to think of another plan. I speak with my landlord, and he suggests that I just change the locks and when she leaves, she can't get back in again. Great idea!! I speak with a local English guy and arrange to meet him at the apartment an hour later.

He arrives and I explain the situation to him. He tells me that he has a bodycam and would he like me for him to put it on.

"Oh yes my man, you're about to see some crazy shit here" I say

We get to the apartment and Alina is about to walk out with her handbag over her shoulder.

"Going somewhere"? I ask

"Yes, I'm going out".

"You are"? "How are you going to get back in if you don't have any keys"?

"Oh yes, I didn't think about that". "I'll just stay in then".

"Ok". I ask. "Last chance". "Do you have the spare keys"?

"No, I don't" she says

I look at Adam, the Locksmith guy and he proceeds to drill.

"What are you doing"? she asks

"I'm changing the locks". "You don't live here and are a guest here". "If you won't give me the spare keys, I'll need to change the locks so when you leave, then you won't be getting back in".

"Well, of course I have the keys" she says

She proceeds to get the keys out of her bag and hands them to me.

"I just want to talk with you alone please Simon" she says

"I have absolutely nothing that I need to say to you Alina".

She walks away and starts mumbling to herself and then it starts.

"Threatening me yes"? "You're threatening me again".

"Nobody is threatening you Alina, you were only asked for the spare keys".

"Yes, threatening me".

Adam and I leave and that is the very last time I see her. I paid Adam for the callout fee and proceeded to head back to Alan and Judith's. My plan now was to wait the two days as the Police advised, chilling at my friends Villa and then head back to the apartment and hopefully she'd be gone.

It's getting close to 8pm now so I decide to head out for some food before heading to Paul and Steve's Villa to chill for the two days. I'm driving along the frontera at the border between Gibraltar and Spain when suddenly, these blue lights start flashing from across the road.

Police literally come from everywhere and surround my car. Shouting and bawling in Spanish. I get dragged out the car and asked for my name and to show my Passport. Once they confirm who I am, they take me to the Police car and an officer that speaks English comes to speak with me.

"There's been an allegation by Alina that you pushed her and grabbed her wrist a few days ago so you will be going to jail tonight Simon".

"What"? I ask. "Is this a joke"?

"It's no joke" replies the officer.

I get taken to the Policia National station in La Linea. Stripped, fingerprinted, photos and DNA taken and put in a cell. They tell me that I'll be going to court in

Algeciras in the morning to answer the allegations. I can't believe it.

I get taken out the cell after about an hour and these two Police officers come in and speak perfect English.

"Hi Simon, what happened with Alina today"?

I told them everything that happened and thankfully not only them but all of the officers in the station believed me after spending most of the day in her company at various stages.

"Congratulations" he says.

"Congratulations"? I ask back very confused

"Yes, congratulations". "She is no longer in your life". "She is very beautiful yes but very crazy". "A good actress my friend so don't you worry about anything".

Don't worry about anything? I'm thinking, is this guy for real man? I'm banged up abroad for absolutely nothing and I've got to spend a night in a cell and go to court in the morning. Again, for absolutely nothing whilst someone I've been nothing but nice to is chilling in my fucking apartment.

I get awakened in the morning and put in a van with everyone else that's going to court. Handcuffed the lot, like I'm some sort of fucking criminal. We arrive at Algeciras court at the back entrance and are taken to a holding cell underneath the court.

There are around thirty other guys in the holding cell, and I stick out like a sore thumb. I'm pretty well groomed. Nice trainers on and a bright yellow t-shirt on. It's full of junkies. Most emptying their nose and their mouths in the corner of the cell every two minutes. It was fucking disgusting.

My normal Spanish Lawyer "Alberto" couldn't represent me today as he was busy with other cases back in La Linea. I spoke to him most of the day the day before, so he was fully aware of everything and briefed up the Lady Lawyer who was taking his place today.

She arrived at the holding cell after about four hours of me being in there. For four hours, I genuinely thought that I was going to be attacked at any point. There were no cameras or guards and anything could've happened. A very scary situation to be in. She comes to the bars and shouts my name.

"Ok Simon, the judge is offering you forty hours community service unpaid work and Alina would also like a four-month restraining order imposed on you also". "If you accept this then the case will be done today".

"You're joking right"? "Her, a restraining order on me ha ha"? "Holy fuck". "I accept nothing". "I've done nothing to that woman except look after her in every single way for three months". "I'm admitting to nothing I haven't done". "Absolutely no way". "Tell the judge I decline his offer thanks".

"Ok Simon, I will tell him". "We shouldn't be long now". "I'll get you in front of him as quick as I can and we'll get you out of here".

"Excellent" I say

The Lawyer heads up the stairs and out of the thirty that was in the cell, I was left until the last two people. Typical. Done absolutely nothing at all and in that holding cell absolutely shitting my pants all day from 10am until 4.30pm when I finally get in front of the judge.

"Simon, yourself and your Lawyer don't accept that Alina's version of events is true". "Is this correct"?

"Oh, absolutely Sir". Completely untrue".

"Ok, you will return on trial on March the 9th 2026 to answer these allegations in court".

"No problem, Sir".

They take the cuffs off me. I sign all the paperwork and get all my stuff back from the Police. Including my shoelaces and my phone etc. They let me out the back gate of the court and I'm finally free. I switch my phone on to let Alan know I'm out and proceed to put my shoelaces back into my trainers.

My phone finally switched on and my laces are done. I phone Alan right away to let him know I'm out. As I start walking away from the court, I see around fifty bags outside the building next door and these two wimmin on the wall next to them. I look to see what the building is. It's a Women's refuge. Those poor women I'm thinking as I call Alan and walk away from the court.

I'm absolutely stinking and need to brush my teeth. I pass the main square in Algeciras on my way to the bus station so decide that I'm going to stop there for a glass of Red Wine on the way as I'm finally a free man.

Or so I thought I was…..

CHAPTER EIGHTEEN
YOU'RE HAVING A LAUGH RIGHT?

I get to the café at Plaza Alta in Algeciras main square and order a glass of Red Wine. As I'm about to sit down, someone shouts my name.

"Simon"!

I look over in the direction of the shout and it's my Spanish Lawyer and friend Alberto. I can't believe it.

He must've just finished his other cases in court that he was at. I had been speaking to him pretty much all of the day before, so he shouts me over. He's sat with another Spanish Gentleman.

"Hey Simon, this is my friend Xavi". "He's a lawyer too".

I say hello and shake Xavi's hand, and the waiter brings over my Wine. I tell Alberto what has been going on since I got arrested last night and I pass him all the paperwork the court gave me, and he can't believe that I've been through what I've been through the past twenty-four hours or so.

He then asks me if he can tell Xavi in Spanish what I've been through the last twenty-four hours and obviously I say yes, so he proceeds to. Xavi is shaking his head as Alberto explains everything.

"So, Simon, what the plan now"? Alberto asks

"Well, I'm absolutely stinking and need to brush my teeth". "I'm just gonna have this Wine and head down to the bus station and get the bus home". "Jump in a nice long shower and probably brush my teeth twenty times ha ha".

"Good idea Simon ha ha" he replies

I literally sit with them for ten minutes. Xavi pays for my Wine, and I bid them farewell. I then head down towards the bus station and can't wait to get home so I can shower. I'm heading to Alan's first who's going to drive me to my car which was abandoned at the Gibraltar border by the Police after I got arrested the night before.

I walk into the bus station and there's quite a few Police officers there. There's about a hundred people in the station waiting for various buses at various platforms and every single officer makes a beeline for me as soon as they see me.

The first two officers approach me. One is male and the other female.

"Nombre"? (Name in Spanish)

"Ermm Simon".

"You need to come with us" says the first officer

"You're having a laugh right"? "I've just got out of fucking jail twenty minutes ago". "I've had a glass of Wine with my Lawyer and came straight here". What the actual fuck"?

"There's been fresh allegations so you will be coming with us".

"Fresh allegations"? "I haven't fucking done anything". "I've just got out of jail". "This is a big fucking mistake here".

"We'll find out at the station Simon" says the officer

We head to Algeciras branch of the Policia National and I get put into a holding room with the female arresting officer stood outside it watching over me. I can't believe this. Surely this is some big misunderstanding.

"Do you speak English"? I ask her

"Yes" she replies

"What is this"? "Is this actually a joke"? "I've just spent twenty-four hours in a cell for nothing and now this shit"?
"You'll find out soon enough" she says

After about ten minutes or so, an officer I recognise from the court earlier walks in.

"Simon" he says

"Yes"

"Have you seen Alina today at all"?

"Noooooooooo". "I've been in fucking jail until 4.30pm". "I walked to Plaza Alta for a glass of Wine with my lawyer and then to the Bus Station". "I haven't seen her since I got my keys off her at my apartment yesterday". "What is this shit"? "I just want to go home and shower".

"Ok Simon, leave it with me and I'll be back".

This is unbelievable. I have absolutely no idea why I'm there or what shit she has come up with now. The arresting officer comes in and basically says that all the shit I went through yesterday, I'll be going through again and going to court again in the morning. I can't believe it. The arresting female officer walks in.

"Simon, you're being arrested today for threatening to kill Alina" she says

"What"! I'm completely stunned. "What"? "When"? "How"?

"Apparently you saw her today and your exact words were". "Today you are going to meet the Devil". "Which in Spain is a threat of death and a threat to kill".

"Saw her today"? "I've been in fucking jail since 8pm last night until 4.30pm just there". "How the fuck have I seen her"? "I mean seriously".

"Apparently you saw her outside the court today and this is what you said to her" she replies

"I haven't fucking seen her". "Please check the CCTV cameras at the court and let me go home". "Holy fuck". "I swear I haven't seen her". "This is so wrong".

I then go through the exact same process I did twenty-four hours earlier and get flung in a cell. I then get transported to the court in the morning and put in the very same holding cell under the court. The same Police Officers are there and can't believe I'm there again.

They all keep coming in. Especially the female officers. Most of them are all coming out with the same remarks.

"Were you with that blonde girl"? "Very beautiful but crazy". She's been walking all round this court the past two days waiting for you".

"What the fuck"?

My Lawyer and my friend Alberto appears at the holding cell around midday to give me some news.

"Ok, the Police have checked all the CCTV and interviewed witnesses and she's lying as I knew and now the judge knows". "You never saw her or spoke to her, but she did see you".

"Wait"! "How"? "I went out the back exit Alberto and then met you five minutes later". "I never saw her man". "Please check if she's outside". "She doesn't know you, but you know her".

"Outside"? "She's been outside since yesterday". "The Police moved her and all her stuff out of your apartment yesterday and dropped her and all of her stuff at the Women's refuge next door".

BOOM!!

All the stuff I saw when I got out of jail yesterday was all hers that was stacked outside the Women's refuge. I never saw her, but she saw me from inside the refuge and went straight next door to the court and made up the death threat. By the time I had finished my Wine, the Police were waiting for me at the Bus station. Unbelievable.

Again, I was one of the last people to get out of the holding cell. The previous night in the cells was absolute madness. Literally junkies in every cell screaming all night to see the doctor for drugs. It was fucking horrific. The holding cell that day wasn't much better. Completely innocent both days and subjected to that pish.

I finally get to go in front of the judge. Two female officers escort me up to the judge. One was the arresting officer from the night before and the other one was the officer who kept coming into the holding cell saying that Alina was crazy. They stop me in the corridor before we go into the judge.

The arresting officer speaks first.

"Simon, I know and every officer in Algeciras and La Linea know that you are completely innocent ok, but this is the Spanish Law unfortunately".

The second female officer.

"Tomorrow, you need to go to La Linea Police station to report her for a false report and harassing you". "We all want her in these cells here".

They take me inside the court in my cuffs yet again. Alberto is there and the judge just looks at me in disbelief again. Shaking his head because he can't believe I'm there again.

"Ok Simon, you are obviously not guilty, and she has been lying". We've done a full investigation already".

"I wouldn't worry too much about your trial in March now either because of this".

"I'm not worried". "I haven't done anything".

The first arresting officer takes the cuffs off me, and I sign all of the paperwork. The Police had to escort me out of the court in case she was waiting for me again to make false allegations, and my Lawyer had to drive his car to the back gate so I could get straight in it for him to drive me home.

All unbelievable really. Three days banged up abroad for absolutely nothing. The main thing is though; she's now out of my life and my apartment now for good. Well, hopefully…..

CHAPTER NINETEEN
WHAT DOES THE FUTURE HOLD?

As you can see, I've had a pretty mad run at it since I got here in the Summer of 2018. Lots of ups and downs but seriously, more ups for sure. I think about that guy that came here in 2018 completely broken and with nothing and do you know what? I'd help that guy out for sure.

Maybe that's why I got into this position recently with Alina. I actually saw a bit of me when I saw the predicament she was in and only wanted to help her and look where that got me ha ha? It won't put me off helping people in the future but a very scary few days all the same.

I've been single for two and half years now and was very happy on my own until she came into my life. It was nice to have a beautiful woman around again but obviously it all went very Pete Tong. I believe I'll find love again one day but certainly not looking for it. What will be will be.

I have a very good job in Gibraltar in the gambling industry and the nightshifts certainly fit into my lifestyle. It's very quiet at night and we work in a very small team so it's very chilled and that's me to a tee.

I own a Celtic Podcast now as well which has been going for just over a year now and it's flying. I enjoy presenting it and have a great bunch of lads that contribute to it as well. The viewers are great craic too and we're all one big family. Hopefully that can be my full-time job in the next year or so if it really takes off.

Then there's my Books. This is book number eight since 2018 so we're still well on track for at least one a year. I enjoy writing, its therapy, believe it or not? Diaries aren't quite the thing these days, so all of these books are my diaries really. I'm a wee bit of most of the characters in my books. I'm sure those that know me will recognise the traits ha ha.

I do get lonely. I chose to move abroad yes and without that support network from back home, it's very difficult.

I was in a very serious car crash when I was seven years old. I had a blood clot removed from my brain and obviously took a very serious bump to the front of my head. I've always wondered lots of things since then about that. Has it affected my life, and I don't even know it?

I've always felt very different since then. Why am I here? Why did I survive? What is my purpose here? Lots of questions really. I always felt that I was going to be somebody and achieve stuff but have I really? I've failed as a dad, a brother, an uncle and a son in my eyes.

The rest of the stuff means nothing really. Moving abroad, having a good job, owning a Podcast and writing books. I'd much rather be successful at the above stuff, but I just haven't been and that really bothers me, it really does.

What does the future hold? Who knows? None of us know do we?

I just hope to be a better guy than I was yesterday. I'm not a bad guy. I just do stupid shit. I can take six months off the booze and then start again and just completely rip the hole out of it and go on a month bender. That's just me and I probably won't change. One shall try though.

I've had the most amazing women in the world since I've been over here and blew it with all of them. I just always seem to push people away from me and I don't know if I actually do it on purpose, so I don't get hurt. Again, I think the car crash has definitely had a lasting impact on me and the future scares me about that.

Is that head injury going to affect me in the future or has it affected me since I've been seven years old? I'm nearly fifty now so I guess we'll never know, and I've had a good innings really, so again, what will be will be. I've lived the life of ten men.

It's very scary writing a book as you're letting complete strangers inside your head, but I've been as honest as I can be in this book. Yes, a few things in it are going to piss a few people off but I'm past the caring stage. I call life as I see it. I say what I see and that won't change.

I still have lots to do personally that I want to achieve and I definitely need to think about my lifestyle choices now as I'm close to that half century.

Yes, I'm all in with everything. I rip the pish out of everything. I go all in with Love, with drinking, with exercise, Food, kindness, generosity and generally everything. That's my personality. I love my own company too.

In my twenties and thirties, I was Jack the lad. Popular and sought attention from everyone. I've completely went full circle since I turned forty. I'd rather be on my own. I barely go out now and I'm the worst person in the world for keeping in touch with anyone.

I'm so lucky as my phone actually doesn't stop. I have so many people that look out for me all over the World and I'm so grateful for that. I have lots of friends and I appreciate them all. I don't get the appeal of this version of me but I'm thankful all the same.

I think the main thing that I want and strive for is peace and tranquillity in my life. We all want that right? I do my best to make sure that happens these days, but God certainly throws a spanner in the works every now and then by throwing me numpties into my life ha ha. Keeps me on my toes.

The whole point of this book really was for a timeline of events for when I arrived in Spain. Also, the truth about everything that's happened, good and bad. I'm not perfect at all or even saying that but I think it's best to get my side of the story out and the truth.

I haven't grown so much in my life as I have in these past seven to eight years. I've literally been on my own. Yes, people have come and gone. Friends and girlfriends etc. I ask myself this though, were they really friends or girlfriends? They're not in your life for a reason, right?

People do come into your life for a reason. They all come into it to teach you a lesson, good or bad. Learn from everyone, that's why God sends them to us. I wish he would slow doon a wee bit with me though ha ha. I need a couple of years break again, I think.

No in all seriousness, by the time this book comes out I will actually be a grandfather and that scares the shite out of me. My seventeen-year-old son will be more scared. He'll say he isn't as he's in that, doesn't give a fuck about anything attitude at the minute. Life is about to change for us all.

I hope that I can be a better part of my children's, my family and my grand-children's lives when they come along. This might sound weird, but I just feel that they are all better off without me. I don't want to bother anyone these days.

It's the same with relationships. I've dated lots of amazing women these past two and half years that I've been single, but I keep making excuses to not go on date number two. People would cut their right arm off to date the women I have but I'm just not interested anymore. I know, I'm daft.

I don't only think about the guy that came here in 2018 to Spain. I think about that wee guy that was brought up in a wee fishing village on the West Coast of Scotland all those years ago. Did I ever think that at forty-seven years old I'd be in an apartment with views of Gibraltar and Morocco?

Honestly? Yes I did.

I had my dreams, and I had my visions early on that I was different. That I was going to be somebody. That I wouldn't stop until I got to that level of peace and tranquillity in my life and that I had a comfortable life with no stress or drama in it.

Lots of things have been sent to try me over the years obviously ha ha but I can honestly say at the time of finishing this book in late 2025, I'm where I want to be barring having my amazing woman, but, she will come eventually.

It's been a blast over the years, and I've tried my best to be a decent guy in life. I think I've achieved that as best I can up until now. I hope to write more books and hopefully live in more countries as I get older. I always get itchy feet. Who knows, maybe even Scotland again one day.

Before I go, I just want to thank a few people. First, my Mother Tina. She has always been the driving force for me. I have always had her no-nonsense attitude about everything. I get my drive and determination from her so thank you Mum. I love you. X

My children Paige and Aiden. It's been a rocky one since 2018. We've mended fences and broken some along the way too. You are now both adults and know where I am the second you need me. Love you both. xx

The last people I want to mention have been the Ladies in my life. My ex-wife Kelly and my three main girlfriends since I've been here, Caroline, Helen and Anna.

Kelly, I'd like to apologise to you for being a shite husband and I wish you all the best for your future.

Caroline. Thanks for teaching me about posh stuff and vision boards ha ha. It was fun but I couldn't afford the lifestyle you require. All the best. x

Helen. I don't know what to say really barring we were 90% there. I think you were too set in your ways with life where you were located. I had a great time with you, and it was a really good laugh. All the best to you. x

Finally, the beautiful and amazing Anna. The love of my life up until now for sure. For someone so young, you taught me so much about life. You had nothing but didn't care because you had me. I know that we had to part. It wasn't our time. I hope you have an amazing life. x

That's me out folks. That's my soul been borne for you all to see. We move on and we push forward always. Hopefully we all have better times to come. Thank you all for your continued support and hopefully there's plenty more books to come also.

I love you all. Cheers. x

Scott. x

Dedication -

This Book is dedicated to Fay Armitage. You'll remember Fay from the very early chapters of this Book. Fay was one of the first people I met when I moved over here, and we were drawn towards each other right away. I was a poor soul at the time, and she noticed that right away and gave me the pep talks and the affection I needed at that time.

Fay was so beautiful and stunning. A woman in her 60's at the time and always dressed well, was nice to everyone and just an all-round amazing human being. She was always perfect. Her hair, her makeup and her lippy ha ha. Always looked a million dollars.

I got the very sad news earlier this year that she had been diagnosed with motor neurone's disease and was now a poor wee soul nearing the end of her life. I contacted her daughter Bethany, and I arranged to go and meet her at her home.

Bethany told me that she had lost her power of speech now and everything and I was going to get a massive shock when I see her now. I had to go and see her. Kindness goes a long way with me and when I needed it the most, she was there for me, so I was certainly going to be there for her.

I went to see her a few months ago and she was indeed a poor wee soul, but her eyes lit up when she saw me and we embraced, and I chatted away to her as much as I could. I kept telling her that she still the most beautiful woman in the world. This book is for you Fay. x

Printed in Dunstable, United Kingdom